LOW & SLOW

COMFORT FOOD FOR COLD NIGHTS

LOW & SLOW

COMFORT FOOD FOR COLD NIGHTS

Louise Franc

Smith
Street
Books

CONTENTS

Introduction

When the temperature cools down and the nights become longer, we tend to crave our favourite comfort foods – slow-cooked meats, rich soups and stews, hearty roasts and fragrant curries. This is the time of year when we skip the salads and quick stir-fries and the art of slow cooking comes into its own.

'Low and slow' refers to the cooking method used in many of the recipes in this book – low temperature cooking for a long period of time, either in the oven or on the stovetop, which helps to add a great depth of flavour and tenderness to dishes. You'll also find that most of the recipes in the book are one-pot classics. The beauty of this is once you've started the cooking process, there's not much more you'll need to do – except relax and let time do all the work for you.

This way of cooking is perfectly suited to particular cuts of meat – lamb and pork shoulder, stewing beef and beef cheeks, bone-in chicken pieces – which all tend to be less expensive than regular cuts. We've added in some fish and seafood dishes too. Although these are much quicker to cook, they are just as flavoursome and comforting as the heartier meat dishes.

Of course, no beautifully slow-cooked meal is complete without something luscious and sweet to finish on. Slow cooking is also a perfect way to cook desserts – think rich chocolatey steamed puddings, warming crumbles and baked fruits.

It's all about slowing down and enjoying the process of cooking again!

NOTES ON THE RECIPES

All the recipes in this book give oven temperatures for fan-forced ovens. If you're using a conventional oven, simply increase the temperature by about 10–20°C/30–50°F.

We have used 20 ml (¾ fl oz) tablespoon measures, which is the equivalent of 4 teaspoons.

SOUP

Classic French Onion Soup

SERVES 6

Heat the olive oil and butter in a large heavy-based saucepan over medium heat. Add the onions and stir to coat in the oil and butter mixture. Reduce the heat to low, then cover and cook for 30 minutes, stirring occasionally.

Stir in the sugar and wine. Cover and cook for a further 30 minutes, stirring occasionally, until the onions are very tender.

Remove the lid and continue to cook, stirring, for another 5–10 minutes, until the onions begin to caramelise and become an even golden brown.

Add the stock and bay leaf, then simmer for another 30 minutes.

Meanwhile, preheat the oven to 160°C/320°F (fan-forced). To make the croutons, lightly brush both sides of each slice of bread with olive oil and place on a baking tray. Bake for 10 minutes on each side, until crunchy and deep golden brown.

Increase the oven temperature to 200°C/400°F (fan forced).

Remove the bay leaf from the soup. Stir in the Cognac, then taste and season with sea salt flakes and freshly ground black pepper.

Pour a small ladle of soup into six ovenproof soup bowls. Add a crouton and a sprinkling of gruyère cheese. Ladle in the remaining soup, then add another crouton to each bowl and a thick layer of cheese.

Place the bowls on a baking tray and carefully transfer to the oven. Bake for about 5 minutes, or until the soup is bubbling hot and the cheese has formed a golden crust.

Allow to stand for a few minutes before serving, as the soup and bowls will be extremely hot.

2 tablespoons olive oil
50 g (1¾ oz) butter
3 brown onions, thinly sliced
3 red onions, thinly sliced
3 white onions, thinly sliced
½ teaspoon soft brown sugar
250 ml (8½ fl oz/1 cup) dry white wine
1 litre (34 fl oz/4 cups) good-quality chicken stock
1 bay leaf
2 tablespoons Cognac, dry vermouth or dry sherry
200 g (7 oz/1½ cups) grated gruyère cheese

CROUTONS
sourdough baguette, cut into 12 thick slices
2 tablespoons olive oil

Fragrant Fish Soup with Pappardelle

SERVES 4

First, prepare the stock. Heat a large heavy-based saucepan over medium heat. Add the olive oil, leek, carrot, garlic, fennel, bay leaves, thyme, salt and orange zest. Cook for 10 minutes, or until softened, stirring occasionally.

Add the tomatoes, as well as the fish heads and bones. Cook, stirring occasionally, for a further 15 minutes. Pour in the vinegar or wine and 750 ml (25½ fl oz/3 cups) water. Heat until simmering, then reduce the heat and cook at a gentle simmer for a further 40 minutes.

Pour the stock through a fine sieve into a large clean saucepan, pressing out as much liquid as you can. Return the stock to a medium–low heat, adjust the seasoning and leave to simmer.

Bring a large saucepan of salted water to the boil. Add the pasta and cook until al dente. Drain, return to the pan, stir the butter through and cover to keep warm.

Add the fish to the hot stock and cook for 2 minutes. Add the mussels and cook for 2 minutes more. Add the scallops, remove the soup from the heat and stir in half the parsley.

Divide the pasta among four soup bowls, then ladle the soup over. Scatter with the remaining parsley and serve with crusty bread.

For best results, avoid using oily fish such as salmon, mackerel and ocean trout in this dish.

200 g (7 oz) pappardelle pasta
1 tablespoon butter
200 g (7 oz) skinless firm white fish fillet, such as snapper, cut into 2 cm (¾ inch) pieces
12 mussels, cleaned
12 scallops
15 g (½ oz/½ cup) finely chopped flat-leaf (Italian) parsley
crusty bread, to serve

STOCK
2 tablespoons olive oil
2 leeks, white and pale green parts only, chopped
2 carrots, chopped
2 garlic cloves, bruised with the back of a knife
1 fennel bulb, sliced
2 bay leaves
3 thyme sprigs
1 teaspoon sea salt flakes
1 strip of orange zest
3 tomatoes, chopped
1.5 kg (3 lb 5 oz) heads and bones of white fish such as cod, flathead, perch, bream, whiting or snapper (see tip), gills removed, cleaned and rinsed
60 ml (2 fl oz/¼ cup) apple cider vinegar, or 250 ml (8½ fl oz/1 cup) dry white wine

Chunky Beetroot & Vegetable Soup

SERVES 4

Heat the olive oil in a large heavy-based saucepan over medium–low heat. Sauté the leek, beetroot, parsnip, carrot, bay leaves, garlic and caraway seeds for 10 minutes, or until the vegetables start to soften, stirring occasionally.

Add the farro and stock. Bring to the boil over high heat, then reduce the heat to low. Cover and simmer for 30 minutes, or until the farro is nearly tender.

Add the cabbage and a little extra water, if necessary. Cover and simmer for a further 10 minutes, or until the vegetables and farro are tender. Season to taste with sea salt flakes and freshly ground black pepper.

Serve with a swirl of sour cream, garnished with dill.

> *Farro is an ancient, highly nutritious wheat grain that has fed the people of the Near East and the Mediterranean for thousands of years. Cracked farro will cook more quickly than whole grains; if you only have whole farro grains, soak them overnight for quicker cooking.*

2 tablespoons olive oil
1 leek, white part only, thinly sliced
2 beetroot (beets), peeled and diced
1 parsnip, peeled and diced
2 carrots, unpeeled, diced
2 bay leaves
4 garlic cloves, thinly sliced
2 teaspoons caraway seeds
100 g (3½ oz/½ cup) cracked farro (see tip) or pearl barley
1 litre (34 fl oz/4 cups) vegetable or chicken stock
150 g (5½ oz/2 cups) finely shredded white or red cabbage
sour cream, to serve
dill sprigs, to garnish

Smoky White Bean & Ham Hock Soup with Gremolata

SERVES 6

Heat the olive oil in a large heavy-based saucepan over medium heat. Add the onion and carrot and cook, stirring, for 5–6 minutes, or until softened. Add the garlic and cook, stirring, for 1 minute.

Add the ham hock, beans, stock and all the paprika. Bring to the boil, then reduce the heat to low. Cover and simmer, stirring occasionally, for 2½ hours, or until the beans and hock are tender.

Remove the hock from the soup, then remove and shred the meat. Discard the skin and bone.

Remove about one-third of the beans and carrots from the soup and mash, then return to the soup with the meat. Taste and season with sea salt flakes and freshly ground black pepper if required.

Combine the gremolata ingredients in a small bowl.

Serve the soup in large bowls, with a sprinkle of gremolata and slices of crusty bread.

1 tablespoon olive oil
1 onion, finely chopped
1 carrot, halved lengthways and
   chopped
3 garlic cloves, crushed
500 g (1 lb 2 oz) smoked ham hock
200 g (7 oz/1 cup) dried cannellini
   beans, rinsed
2 litres (68 fl oz/8 cups) vegetable
   stock
2 teaspoons sweet paprika
2 teaspoons smoked paprika
crusty bread, to serve

GREMOLATA
zest of 1 lemon
1 long red chilli, finely chopped
15 g (½ oz/½ cup) finely chopped
   flat-leaf (Italian) parsley

Ethiopian-Style Lentil & Tomato Soup

SERVES 6

Combine all the Berbere spice mix ingredients in a small bowl, mixing well. Set aside in a small airtight container.

Heat the olive oil in a large saucepan over medium heat. Add the onion, carrot and celery. Cover and cook for 10 minutes, stirring occasionally, until softened but not browned. If the vegetables begin to stick and brown before they are softened, add a tablespoon of water.

Add the garlic and 2 tablespoons of the spice mix and cook, stirring, for a further minute, or until fragrant.

Stir in the tomatoes, lentils and stock. Bring to a simmer, then cover and reduce the heat to low. Simmer for 30–40 minutes, or until the lentils are tender.

Add the potato and cook for a further 10 minutes. Stir in the lemon juice.

Combine the topping ingredients in a small bowl. Serve the soup in individual bowls, with a spoonful of the zesty yoghurt on top.

The Berbere spice mix makes more than you need for this recipe, but is useful to have on hand as a ready-made seasoning for other dishes. Store the remainder in an airtight container in the fridge and use in your next batch of soup, or to season roast chicken, steak or vegetables. It is best used within 3 months.

2 tablespoons olive oil
1 brown onion, finely chopped
2 carrots, diced
3 celery stalks, halved lengthways and chopped
2 garlic cloves, crushed
2 tablespoons Berbere spice mix (from below; see tip)
400 g (14 oz) tinned crushed tomatoes
185 g (6½ oz/1 cup) brown lentils, or 250 g (9 oz/1 cup) red lentils, rinsed
2 litres (68 fl oz/8 cups) vegetable stock
1 potato, diced
2 tablespoons lemon juice

BERBERE SPICE MIX
⅛ teaspoon ground cloves
⅛ teaspoon ground allspice
¼ teaspoon ground nutmeg
½ teaspoon ground coriander
½ teaspoon ground fenugreek
½ teaspoon freshly ground black pepper
1 teaspoon ground cinnamon
1 teaspoon ground cardamom
1 teaspoon ground ginger
2 teaspoons chilli flakes
1 tablespoon cayenne pepper
2 tablespoons hot paprika
1 tablespoon sweet paprika

ZESTY YOGHURT TOPPING
90 g (3 oz/⅓ cup) plain yoghurt
3 tablespoons finely chopped flat-leaf (Italian) parsley
zest of ½ lemon

Tuscan Chicken Soup

SERVES 6

Preheat the oven to 160°C/320°F (fan-forced). Line a baking tray with baking paper.

Brush the chicken thighs with olive oil and sprinkle with sea salt flakes and freshly ground black pepper. Place on the lined baking tray and bake for 25 minutes. Remove from the oven and rest for 10 minutes.

Meanwhile, heat a little olive oil in a large saucepan over medium heat and sauté the onion, carrot and celery for 10 minutes. Add the garlic, zucchini and rosemary and cook for a further 5 minutes.

Stir in the tomatoes, stock, oregano and basil, then simmer over low heat for 40 minutes.

Bring 2 litres (68 fl oz/8 cups) salted water to the boil in a saucepan over high heat. Cook the pasta shells until almost al dente, then drain.

Remove the chicken meat from the bones and cut into 2 cm (¾ inch) pieces. Add the pasta, chicken meat and any juices from the baking tray to the soup and simmer for a final 5 minutes.

Serve in deep bowls, scattered with the grated cheese.

6 skinless chicken thighs, bone in
olive oil, for brushing and pan-frying
1 brown onion, finely diced
2 carrots, finely diced
3 celery stalks, finely diced
2 garlic cloves, crushed
2 zucchini (courgettes), diced
2 tablespoons chopped rosemary
400 g (14 oz) tinned crushed
   tomatoes
1 litre (34 fl oz/4 cups) chicken stock
2 teaspoons finely chopped oregano,
   or 1 teaspoon dried
2 teaspoons finely chopped basil, or
   1 teaspoon dried
45 g (1½ oz/½ cup) small pasta shells
grated Pecorino Romano or parmesan
   cheese, to serve

Clam Chowder

Place the clams in a large saucepan. Pour in the wine and 250 ml (8½ fl oz/1 cup) water. Cover and cook over medium heat for about 10 minutes, or until the clams have opened.

Line a sieve with muslin (cheesecloth) or paper towel and set it over a bowl. Strain the clam broth through the sieve to remove any sand or grit from the clams; reserve the cooking broth in the bowl.

When cool enough to handle, remove the clams from the shells. Discard the shells, and roughly chop any large clams. Set the clams and the broth aside separately.

Place the kaiserfleisch and 125 ml (4 fl oz/½ cup) water in a large heavy-based saucepan over medium heat. Cook, stirring occasionally, for about 10 minutes, until the water has evaporated, the pork fat renders and the meat begins to crisp. Remove the bacon using a slotted spoon and add to the reserved clams.

Add the butter, leek, celery and bay leaf to the pan and cook, stirring, for 8 minutes, or until the leek has softened.

Add the reserved clam broth, milk and potatoes. Season with sea salt flakes and freshly ground black pepper and simmer gently for 15 minutes, or until the potato is cooked and starting to break down.

Remove 500 ml (17 fl oz/2 cups) liquid from the soup, along with about 115 g (4 oz/½ cup) of cooked vegetables. Cool slightly, then use a stick mixer to blend until smooth.

Return the blended liquid to the soup. Stir in the cream, reserved bacon and clams. Adjust the seasoning and gently reheat until simmering.

Serve in deep soup bowls, sprinkled with the parsley.

2 kg (4 lb 6 oz) fresh clams, scrubbed clean

125 ml (4 fl oz/½ cup) dry white wine

150 g (5½ oz) kaiserfleisch or thickly cut bacon, cut into 1 cm (½ inch) cubes

1 tablespoon butter

1 leek, white part only, cut in half lengthways, then sliced

2 celery stalks, chopped

1 bay leaf

750 ml (25½ fl oz/3 cups) full-cream milk

2 russet or other floury potatoes, peeled and cut into 2 cm (¾ inch) cubes

185 ml (6½ fl oz/¾ cup) pouring (single/light) cream

15 g (½ oz/½ cup) finely chopped flat-leaf (Italian) parsley

Mushroom & Barley Soup

SERVES 4

Heat the olive oil in a large heavy-based saucepan over medium heat. Add the leek and cook, covered, stirring occasionally, for 5 minutes, or until starting to soften.

Add the mushrooms. Cover the pan and cook, stirring occasionally, for 5 minutes, or until they start to release their juices. Add the garlic and tomato paste and cook, stirring, for a further minute.

Tie the thyme and parsley together with kitchen string. Add to the pan with the carrot, celery, barley and stock. Cover and bring to the boil, then reduce the heat to low. Simmer, partially covered, for 35–40 minutes, or until the barley is tender.

Add a little boiling water to adjust the consistency to your liking. Season to taste with sea salt flakes and freshly ground black pepper.

Remove the tied herb bundle, stripping the thyme leaves from the stalks and stirring them into the soup. Serve with crusty bread.

Soaking the barley overnight in water will reduce the cooking time.

1 tablespoon olive oil
1 leek, white part only, thinly sliced
300 g (10½ oz) small portobello or Swiss brown mushrooms, thinly sliced
2 garlic cloves, crushed
2 tablespoons tomato paste (concentrated purée)
4 thyme sprigs
6 flat-leaf (Italian) parsley stalks
2 carrots, diced
2 celery stalks, sliced
200 g (7 oz/1 cup) pearl barley, rinsed
1.25 litres (42 fl oz/5 cups) chicken stock
crusty bread, to serve

Borlotti Bean & Bacon Soup with Basil Oil

SERVES 4

Put the beans in a large bowl, cover with plenty of cold water and soak overnight. Drain and set aside.

Cook the bacon in a large saucepan over high heat for 2–3 minutes, until lightly browned. Add the olive oil, onion, carrot and celery and cook over medium heat for 5 minutes, or until the vegetables are lightly browned and just softened. Add the garlic, rosemary, bay leaves and tomato paste and cook, stirring, for 1–2 minutes.

Add the beans, potatoes, stock and 1 litre (34 fl oz/4 cups) water. Partially cover and bring to a simmer. Cook, partially covered, over low heat for 1 hour, removing any scum that rises to the surface. Allow to cool slightly.

Remove the bay leaves and strip the rosemary sprigs, discarding the stems and returning the leaves to the soup. Season to taste with sea salt flakes and freshly ground black pepper.

Combine the basil oil ingredients in a small food processor with a small pinch of salt. Blend to a smooth purée.

Blend the soup roughly using a stick blender, or transfer in two batches to a food processor and blend until just smooth, with some vegetables and beans still remaining quite whole.

Gently reheat the soup. Ladle into bowls, drizzle with the basil oil and serve with crusty bread.

If you prefer a slightly thicker soup, increase the potato to 400 g (14 oz), or add a small handful of short pasta (such as ditalini) with the beans and simmer it in the soup.

250 g (9 oz/1¼ cups) dried borlotti (cranberry) beans
100 g (3½ oz) diced bacon
2 tablespoons olive oil
1 large onion, finely chopped
2 carrots, chopped
2 celery stalks, chopped
3 garlic cloves, finely chopped
2 rosemary sprigs
2 bay leaves
1 tablespoon tomato paste (concentrated purée)
2 potatoes, peeled and chopped
1 litre (34 fl oz/4 cups) vegetable stock
crusty bread, to serve

BASIL OIL
25 g (1 oz/½ cup, firmly packed) basil leaves
1 small garlic clove, peeled
60 ml (2 fl oz/¼ cup) olive oil

Caribbean-Style Black Bean Soup

SERVES 4

Put the beans in a large bowl, cover with plenty of cold water and soak overnight. Drain and set aside.

Heat the olive oil in a large heavy-based saucepan over medium heat. Sauté the celery, carrot and leek, stirring occasionally, for 10–12 minutes, or until softened. Add the garlic, jalapeño chilli and spices and cook, stirring, until fragrant. Stir in the tomato paste and cook for 2 minutes.

Add the beans and 1 litre (34 fl oz/4 cups) water. Increase the heat to high and bring to the boil, then reduce the heat to medium. Simmer, partially covered, for 1¼ hours, stirring occasionally, and adding a little more water if the mixture starts to dry out.

Add the tomatoes and sweet potato and simmer for a further 30 minutes, or until the beans are soft.

Season to taste with sea salt flakes and freshly ground black pepper, then stir in the coriander.

Serve with sour cream, lime wedges and corn bread.

220 g (8 oz/1 cup) dried black beans
1 tablespoon olive oil
2 celery stalks, chopped
2 carrots, chopped
1 leek, white part only, finely sliced
3 garlic cloves, crushed
1 jalapeño chilli, seeded and finely chopped
1 teaspoon smoked paprika
½ teaspoon ground allspice
60 g (2 oz/¼ cup) tomato paste (concentrated purée)
400 g (14 oz) tinned crushed tomatoes
1 orange sweet potato, peeled and diced
large handful of coriander (cilantro) leaves and stalks, chopped
sour cream or plain yogurt, to serve
1 lime, cut into wedges
corn bread, to serve

VEGETARIAN

Stuffed Poblanos

SERVES 4

Preheat the oven to 150°C/300°F (fan-forced). Lightly grease a
20 cm x 30 cm (8 inch x 12 inch) baking dish.

To make the sauce, heat the olive oil in a saucepan over medium heat
and sauté the onion and sweet potato for about 5 minutes, stirring
occasionally. Add the garlic and jalapeño chilli and cook for a further
2 minutes. Add the passata, salt and oregano and simmer over low
heat for 10 minutes.

Meanwhile, start preparing the filling. In a small saucepan, bring the
quinoa and 250 ml (8½ fl oz/1 cup) water to the boil over medium
heat. Reduce the heat to low, then cover and simmer for 15 minutes.
Drain off any excess liquid and place in a large mixing bowl with the
corn, beans, feta and coriander. Sprinkle the cumin and lime juice
over and mix together well.

Leaving the stems intact, cut the poblano chillies in half lengthways,
removing the ribs and seeds. Evenly divide the filling mixture among
the poblano halves.

Pour the tomato sauce mixture into the baking dish. Add the poblano
halves, placing them in the baking dish, open side up.

Cover the dish tightly with baking paper, then foil. Transfer to the
oven and bake for 1 hour.

Remove the foil and baking paper. Sprinkle the mozzarella over the
poblano halves and bake for a further 20 minutes, or until the cheese
has melted. Allow to cool a little before serving.

*If you can't find poblano chillies, use small red capsicums
(bell peppers) instead.*

4 large poblano chillies (see tip)
75 g (2½ oz/½ cup) grated mozzarella

FILLING
100 g (3½ oz/½ cup) quinoa, rinsed
3 corn cobs, kernels removed
400 g (14 oz) tinned black beans,
  rinsed and drained
150 g (5½ oz/1 cup) crumbled feta
25 g (1 oz/½ cup) chopped coriander
  (cilantro) leaves
1 teaspoon ground cumin
juice of 1 lime

SAUCE
2 tablespoons olive oil
1 small onion, finely chopped
1 small sweet potato, grated
2 garlic cloves, crushed
1 jalapeño chilli, seeds removed,
  finely chopped
700 ml (23½ fl oz) tomato passata
1 teaspoon sea salt flakes
¼ teaspoon dried oregano

Pumpkin, Silverbeet & Tofu Curry

SERVES 4

Heat half the peanut oil in a large heavy-based saucepan over medium heat. Add the tofu, mustard seeds and turmeric and gently stir-fry for 1–2 minutes, or until the tofu is well coated and lightly browned. Remove the tofu from the pan and set aside.

Add the remaining oil to the pan, along with the silverbeet stalks. Stir, then cover and cook over medium–low heat for 3–5 minutes, or until just tender, stirring occasionally. Add the garlic, ginger and curry powder and cook, stirring, for another 1–2 minutes, or until fragrant.

Now add the pumpkin, carrot and stock. Bring to a simmer, then cover and leave to cook for 10 minutes.

Stir in the cauliflower and silverbeet leaves, cover and cook for 6 minutes.

Return the tofu to the pan, stir gently, and add the snow peas and coconut milk. Cook, uncovered, for a final 5 minutes, or until the tofu is heated through and the cauliflower is tender. As the pumpkin cooks it will start to break down a little, thickening the sauce slightly.

Serve with steamed rice, scattered with coriander.

2 tablespoons peanut oil
200 g (7 oz) firm tofu, cut into 2 cm (¾ inch) cubes
1 teaspoon black mustard seeds
½ teaspoon ground turmeric
500 g (1 lb 2 oz) silverbeet (Swiss chard), stalks thinly sliced, leaves shredded
2 garlic cloves, crushed
3 cm (1¼ inch) piece of fresh ginger, peeled and finely grated
1 tablespoon curry powder
500 g (1 lb 2 oz) pumpkin (winter squash), peeled, seeded and cut into 4 cm (1½ inch) pieces
2 carrots, cut into strips
500 ml (17 fl oz/2 cups) vegetable stock
200 g (7 oz) cauliflower, cut into florets
100 g (3½ oz) snow peas (mangetout), trimmed
185 ml (6½ fl oz/¾ cup) coconut milk
steamed white rice, to serve
handful of coriander (cilantro) sprigs, to garnish

Slow-Cooked Baked Beans

SERVES 4

Put the beans in a large bowl and sprinkle with the salt. Cover with plenty of cold water and leave to soak for 8 hours, or overnight.

The next day, preheat the oven to 140°C/275°F (fan-forced).

Drain the beans, place in a saucepan and cover with cold water. Bring to the boil, then reduce the heat and simmer for 10 minutes. Drain, rinse with cold water and set aside.

Heat the olive oil in a large flameproof casserole dish over medium heat. Add the onion, garlic, carrot and celery and cook, stirring, for 10 minutes. Add the drained beans, bay leaf and paprika, and mix.

Stir in the tomatoes, passata, salt flakes, sugar and vinegar. Add 2 litres (68 fl oz/8 cups) water, or enough to generously cover the beans by 10 cm (4 inches).

Bring the mixture to a gentle boil, then cover the pan with a sheet of baking paper. Put the lid on and carefully transfer to the oven. Bake for 2 hours.

Check the beans and give the mixture a stir. The sauce should be a little runny, but starting to thicken; if it looks dry, add a little water. Return to the oven and bake for a further 1 hour, or until the beans are tender, in a rich, thick, glossy sauce.

Serve for breakfast, lunch or dinner, alongside eggs on sourdough toast, or with salad.

400 g (14 oz/2 cups) dried haricot, cannellini or borlotti (cranberry) beans
2 tablespoons salt
60 ml (2 fl oz/¼ cup) extra virgin olive oil
2 red onions, finely chopped
2 garlic cloves, finely chopped
1 carrot, chopped
2 celery stalks, diced
1 bay leaf
2 teaspoons sweet paprika
400 g (14 oz) tinned crushed tomatoes
185 ml (6½ fl oz/¾ cup) tomato passata
1½ teaspoons sea salt flakes
2 tablespoons dark muscovado sugar
60 ml (2 fl oz/¼ cup) cider vinegar

Roasted Pumpkin Risotto with Browned Butter, Sage, Orange & Pine Nuts

SERVES 4

Preheat the oven to 170°C/340°F (fan-forced). Line a baking tray with baking paper.

Put the pumpkin in a large bowl. Drizzle with 1½ tablespoons of the olive oil, sprinkle generously with sea salt flakes and freshly ground black pepper and toss to combine. Place on the lined baking tray and roast for 30 minutes, or until golden.

Pour the stock into a saucepan and bring just to the boil. Turn off the heat.

In a large shallow saucepan or deep frying pan, heat the remaining olive oil and a third of the butter. Cook the onion over low heat for 5 minutes, or until softened. Add the garlic, bay leaf, thyme sprigs and rice, stirring to coat the rice in the oil.

Stir in the wine. Gradually add the hot stock, a ladleful at a time, stirring until the stock has been almost absorbed. Keep adding the stock gradually, cooking over low heat.

Stir in the pumpkin with the last addition of stock, mashing it lightly as you stir. Remove the bay leaf and thyme sprigs, discarding the bay leaf, and stripping the leaves off the thyme and adding them back into the risotto. Stir the spinach through.

Melt the remaining butter in a separate frying pan over medium heat. Allow it to foam, then add the pine nuts and sage, swirling the pan as the butter and nuts become golden and start to smell nutty, and the sage becomes a little crispy. Add the orange zest, swirling to heat it through, then immediately pour the butter mixture over the risotto.

Season to taste and serve sprinkled with plenty of grated parmesan.

600 g (1 lb 5 oz) butternut or kent pumpkin (winter squash), peeled and cut into 2 cm (¾ inch) chunks
2½ tablespoons olive oil
1.25 litres (42 fl oz/5 cups) vegetable or chicken stock
75 g (2½ oz) butter
1 onion, finely chopped
2 large garlic cloves, finely chopped
1 bay leaf
2 thyme sprigs
330 g (11½ oz/1½ cups) arborio rice
125 ml (4 fl oz/½ cup) dry white wine
large handful of baby English spinach leaves
40 g (1½ oz/¼ cup) pine nuts or crushed walnuts
small handful of sage leaves
2 teaspoons orange zest
finely grated parmesan, to serve

Baked Eggplant Parmigiana

SERVES 4–6

To make the sugo, heat the olive oil in a saucepan over medium–low heat. Add the onion and cook gently for 10 minutes, stirring occasionally, and adding a little water if it starts to brown. Add the garlic and chilli flakes and cook for a minute further.

Stir in the tomatoes, passata, vinegar, salt, basil and 125 ml (4 fl oz/½ cup) water. Bring to a low boil, then cover and simmer over low heat for 15 minutes, or until the mixture has reduced and thickened to a saucy consistency.

Meanwhile, preheat the oven to 150°C/300°F (fan-forced). Lightly grease a 20 cm (8 inch) square baking dish.

Heat a large heavy-based frying pan over medium–high heat. Brush some of the eggplant slices with some of the olive oil and cook on each side for 1 minute, or until golden brown. Remove to a plate lined with paper towel and finish cooking the remaining eggplant slices.

Lay some of the eggplant slices in the baking dish, in a single layer. Spread a cupful of the sugo over the top. Repeat with more eggplant and sugo layers, finishing with the sugo. Scatter the mozzarella over the top. Cover the dish with foil, transfer to the oven and bake for 1 hour.

Remove the dish from the oven and remove the foil. To make the topping, toss the breadcrumbs and olive oil together in a small bowl, scatter evenly over the bake, then sprinkle with the parmesan. Bake for a further 30 minutes, or until the topping is crunchy and golden.

Remove from the oven and allow to stand for 5 minutes. Serve scattered with basil leaves.

For this recipe, choose fresh glossy small eggplants, as they will not need salting to draw out any bitter juices.

1.5 kg (3 lb 5 oz) eggplants (aubergines), sliced 5 mm (¼ inch) thick
125 ml (4 fl oz/½ cup) olive oil
75 g (2½ oz/½ cup) grated mozzarella
fresh basil leaves, to garnish

SUGO
2 tablespoons olive oil
1 red onion, finely chopped
2 garlic cloves, crushed
¼ teaspoon chilli flakes
400 g (14 oz) tinned crushed tomatoes
500 ml (17 fl oz/2 cups) tomato passata
2 teaspoons balsamic vinegar
1 teaspoon sea salt flakes
2 basil sprigs

TOPPING
15 g (½ oz/¼ cup) panko breadcrumbs
1 tablespoon olive oil
25 g (1 oz/¼ cup) finely grated parmesan

Sri Lankan Dhal Curry

Place the lentils in a heavy-based saucepan with the cinnamon stick, garlic, turmeric and salt. Add 1 litre (34 fl oz/4 cups) water and bring to the boil over medium heat. Reduce the heat to low and simmer, stirring occasionally, for 20–25 minutes, or until the lentils are almost tender; add a little more water if the mixture starts to stick.

Stir in the coconut milk and return to a simmer. Cook for a further 5–10 minutes, or the lentils are tender. Remove from the heat and cover to keep warm.

To prepare the spice oil, heat the peanut oil in a heavy-based frying pan over medium heat. Add the mustard seeds and, when they start to pop, add the cumin and fenugreek seeds. Cook for a further 30 seconds, then add the onion, curry leaves and chilli. Cook, stirring, for 2–3 minutes, or until the onion has softened slightly. Add the tomato and cook for a further 2 minutes, or until the tomato has just softened.

Pour the dhal into a serving dish. Drizzle with the spice oil, garnish with coriander and serve with rice or roti.

400 g (14 oz) red lentils, well rinsed
1 cinnamon stick
3 garlic cloves, crushed
1½ teaspoons ground turmeric
½ teaspoon sea salt flakes
80 ml (2½ fl oz/⅓ cup) coconut milk
coriander (cilantro) leaves, to garnish
steamed white rice or warm roti,
  to serve

SPICE OIL
2 tablespoons peanut oil
½ teaspoon black mustard seeds
½ teaspoon cumin seeds
½ teaspoon fenugreek seeds
1 onion, thinly sliced
small handful of fresh curry leaves
1–2 long green chillies, thinly sliced
1 tomato, chopped

FISH & SEAFOOD

Whole Snapper Baked in a Salt Crust with Saffron Mayonnaise

SERVES 4

Preheat the oven to 180°C/350°F (fan-forced).

Put the cooking salt in a large bowl. Add 250 ml (8½ fl oz/1 cup) water and mix together well.

On a large baking tray, form half the salt mixture into a fish shape, just larger than the snapper. Sit the fish on top. Place the lemon and lime slices into the cavity of the snapper, along with the bay leaves, dill and parsley. Press the remaining salt mixture over the fish, covering and sealing the fish completely.

Transfer to the oven and bake for 30 minutes.

Meanwhile, prepare the saffron mayonnaise. Soak the saffron threads in 1 tablespoon hot water for 15 minutes. In a bowl, combine the egg yolks, mustard, vinegar, salt and pepper. Whisk a few drops of the olive oil into the mixture. Continue adding small amounts of the oil, whisking well after each addition, until all the oil has been incorporated. Stir in the saffron threads and water, then taste and adjust the seasoning if required.

Remove the fish from the oven. Tap around the edge of the salt crust with the tip of a knife to loosen it, then lift the top off.

Transfer the snapper to a platter. Serve immediately, with steamed potatoes, a green salad and the saffron mayonnaise.

1 kg (2 lb 3 oz) cooking salt
1.2 kg (2 lb 10 oz) whole snapper
1 lemon, sliced
1 lime, sliced
2 bay leaves
handful of dill sprigs
handful of flat-leaf (Italian) parsley
  leaves
steamed new potatoes, to serve
green salad, to serve

SAFFRON MAYONNAISE
pinch of saffron threads
2 large free-range egg yolks
½ teaspoon dijon mustard
1 teaspoon cider vinegar
½ teaspoon sea salt flakes
pinch of freshly ground black pepper
250 ml (8½ fl oz/1 cup) light olive oil

Coconut Fish Curry

Place the garlic, ginger, lime zest, lemongrass, coriander roots and chillies in a food processor and process to a coarse paste.

Heat the coconut oil in a wok over high heat and cook the spice paste for a minute or so, until fragrant. Add the coconut milk and palm sugar, reduce the heat to medium, and heat until simmering.

Add the fish and cook for 5 minutes, then stir in the fish sauce, lime juice and lime leaves. Remove from the heat.

Serve the curry in deep bowls on a bed of jasmine rice, garnished with the spring onion and reserved coriander leaves.

SERVES 4

4 garlic cloves, peeled
3 cm (1¼ inch) piece of fresh ginger, peeled
zest of 1 lime
3 lemongrass stems, white bases only, chopped
12 coriander (cilantro) roots, scrubbed clean (reserve the leaves for garnishing)
2 small red chillies, stems removed
1 teaspoon coconut oil
500 ml (17 fl oz/2 cups) coconut milk
½ teaspoon palm sugar (jaggery)
700 g (1 lb 9 oz) skinless firm white fish, cut into 5 cm (2 inch) chunks
2 teaspoons fish sauce
1 tablespoon lime juice
4 kaffir lime leaves, thinly sliced
steamed jasmine rice, to serve
3 spring onions (scallions), thinly sliced

Greek-Style
Slow-Cooked Octopus

SERVES 4

Preheat the oven to 150°C/300°F (fan-forced).

To clean the octopus, use a sharp knife to separate the head from the tentacles, just below the eyes. Cut above the eyes, discard the eye segment, then remove and discard the contents of the head sac. Remove the beak from the centre of the body, where the tentacles join. Turn the head sac inside out and rinse it and the tentacles thoroughly.

Place the octopus in a large flameproof casserole dish. Add the wine, then cover and cook over high heat for 10 minutes. Remove the pan from the heat. Carefully lift the octopus onto a chopping board, retaining the cooking juices in the pan, and leave to cool.

To the cooking juices in the pan, add the olive oil, garlic, red onion and pearl onions. Cook over medium heat for 10 minutes, stirring occasionally.

Cut the octopus tentacles into 5 cm (2 inch) pieces, then add to the pan with the rest of the octopus. Add the vinegar, tomatoes, bay leaves, rosemary, allspice, peppercorns and salt.

Transfer to the oven and bake for 90 minutes, or until the octopus is very tender.

Garnish with parsley and serve with fresh crusty bread.

1 octopus, weighing about 1 kg (2 lb 3 oz)
125 ml (4 fl oz/½ cup) dry white wine
80 ml (2½ fl oz/⅓ cup) olive oil
3 garlic cloves, crushed
1 red onion, finely chopped
300 g (10½ oz) pearl (baby) onions, peeled
1 tablespoon white wine vinegar
3 tomatoes, peeled and chopped
2 bay leaves
1 rosemary sprig
3 allspice berries
1 teaspoon peppercorns
2 teaspoons sea salt flakes
flat-leaf (Italian) parsley leaves, to garnish
crusty bread, to serve

Tuna Pasta Bake with Mushroom, Thyme & Kale

SERVES 4

Preheat the oven to 140°C/275°F (fan-forced).

Bring a large saucepan of salted water to the boil over high heat. Add the macaroni and cook for 9 minutes, or until almost al dente; it will cook further in the oven. Drain the macaroni, reserving 60 ml (2 fl oz/¼ cup) of the cooking water.

Heat a large saucepan over medium heat. Add the olive oil, garlic and mushrooms and cook, stirring, for 4 minutes. Add the kale, thyme, salt and a good pinch of freshly ground black pepper. Cook, stirring, for a further 4 minutes, then remove from the heat.

Stir in the tuna, crème fraîche, cheddar and cooked macaroni, along with the reserved cooking water. Pour the mixture into a baking dish.

To make the topping, combine the sourdough crumbs and olive oil in a small bowl. Toss to coat the bread in the oil, then add the parmesan and mix together. Sprinkle the crumbs over the macaroni mixture and bake for 30 minutes, or until the crumbs are golden brown.

Scatter with the parsley and serve with a green salad.

The advantage of using crème fraîche in recipes such as this is that it is far less likely to split during cooking than cream.

400 g (14 oz) macaroni
2 tablespoons olive oil
1 garlic clove, finely chopped
250 g (9 oz) Swiss brown or portobello mushrooms, sliced
½ bunch kale, finely chopped
6 thyme sprigs, leaves picked
½ teaspoon sea salt flakes
2 x 185 g (6½ oz) tins of tuna in springwater, drained
200 g (7 oz) crème fraîche, light sour cream or pouring (single/light) cream (see tip)
60 g (2 oz/½ cup) grated cheddar
3 tablespoons finely chopped flat-leaf (Italian) parsley
green salad, to serve

TOPPING
1 slice sourdough bread, broken roughly into crumbs
2 teaspoons olive oil
25 g (1 oz/¼ cup) grated parmesan

Confit Salmon with Shaved Fennel & Orange Salad

SERVES 4

Preheat the oven to 100°C/210°F (fan-forced).

Pour the light olive oil into a 20 cm (8 inch) square baking dish. Add the bay leaves, lemon peel strips and thyme sprigs. Place the dish in the oven for 30 minutes, to gently warm the oil and allow the herb flavours to infuse.

Carefully place the salmon fillets into the oil. Bake for 14–15 minutes, then remove the dish from the oven.

Lift the salmon pieces onto a plate lined with paper towel, leaving the salmon to drain. Warm four plates in the residual heat of the oven.

To prepare the salad, combine the fennel, rocket, spinach and orange and lemon segments in a large bowl. Dress with the sea salt flakes and extra virgin olive oil and toss.

Place a salmon fillet on each warm plate and pile the salad on top. Serve immediately.

1 litre (34 fl oz/4 cups) light olive oil
2 bay leaves
3 strips of lemon peel
4 thyme sprigs
4 x 200 g (7 oz) skinless salmon fillets
2 baby fennel bulbs, shaved
90 g (3 oz/2 cups) baby rocket (arugula) leaves
50 g (1¾ oz/1 cup, firmly packed) baby English spinach leaves
2 oranges, segmented (see tip)
1 lemon, segmented (see tip)
pinch of sea salt flakes
2 teaspoons extra virgin olive oil

To segment citrus fruit, place it on a chopping board and carefully cut off the top and bottom, using a sharp knife. Sit the fruit on the chopping board, so it has a flat, stable base. Working your way all around the fruit, using downward strokes and following the curved shape, cut away the peel and all the bitter white pith. Working with one citrus segment at a time, cut closely to the white membrane on each side of the segment, to release each fruit segment, reserving any juices for dressing the salad.

CHICKEN & DUCK

French-Style Chicken Casserole

SERVES 4

Preheat the oven to 130°C/265°F (fan-forced).

Season the chicken with sea salt flakes and freshly ground black pepper. Heat the butter and half the olive oil in a large heavy-based casserole dish. Working in batches if necessary, brown the chicken on both sides over high heat, then remove to a plate.

Add the remaining oil to the dish, then cook the shallot, garlic, carrot and mushrooms over medium heat for 5 minutes. Add the bay leaves, thyme sprigs and wine and simmer for 2 minutes.

Stir in the stock and bring to the boil. Return the chicken pieces to the dish, put the lid on, then place in the oven. Bake for 1½ hours.

Remove the dish from the oven. Add the potato and tarragon, then replace the lid and cook on the stove over low heat for 5–7 minutes, or until the potato is tender. Add the peas and simmer for 2–3 minutes, or until the peas are tender, but still bright green.

Remove and discard the bay leaves. Pick the leaves from the thyme sprigs and add them to the casserole. Garnish with parsley and serve with crusty bread.

4 free-range chicken thigh cutlets, skin on
4 free-range chicken drumsticks
25 g (1 oz) butter
2 tablespoons olive oil
4 French shallots, chopped
2 garlic cloves, finely chopped
1 carrot, cut in half lengthways, then thickly sliced
200 g (7 oz) portobello or Swiss brown mushrooms, quartered
2 bay leaves
3 thyme sprigs
250 ml (8½ fl oz/1 cup) riesling or dry white wine
375 ml (12½ fl oz/1½ cups) chicken stock
200 g (7 oz) potatoes, peeled and cut into small cubes
1 teaspoon tarragon leaves
80 g (2¾ oz/½ cup) freshly podded peas
chopped flat-leaf (Italian) parsley, to garnish
crusty bread, to serve

Panang Chicken Curry

Start by making the spice paste. Place the peanuts and chillies in a heatproof bowl and cover with boiling water. Soak for 10 minutes, then drain and set aside.

Heat a small dry frying pan over medium heat and toast the coriander seeds, cumin seeds, cardamom pod and salt for a minute or two until fragrant, stirring so the spices don't burn.

Place the toasted spices into a mortar and grind them using a pestle. Add the drained peanuts and chillies, along with the galangal, lemongrass, lime leaves and coriander root. Pound until a smooth paste forms, then add the shallot, garlic and shrimp paste and pound again until smooth.

Heat a wok over medium heat and add the peanut oil and spice paste. Fry for a minute or so, stirring often, until fragrant. Add the chicken and stir-fry for 2 minutes, then add the carrot and capsicum and stir-fry for a further minute.

Stir in the coconut milk and tomato wedges and leave to simmer for 5 minutes.

Remove from the heat, then stir in the lime juice and basil leaves. Serve over jasmine rice.

SERVES 4

1 tablespoon peanut oil
500 g (1 lb 2 oz) boneless, skinless chicken thighs, sliced very thinly
1 carrot, thinly sliced on the diagonal
1 small red capsicum (bell pepper), quartered and sliced
250 ml (8½ fl oz/1 cup) coconut milk
2 tomatoes, cut into wedges
juice of ½ lime
3 Thai basil sprigs, leaves picked
steamed jasmine rice, to serve

SPICE PASTE
40 g (1½ oz/¼ cup) raw peanuts
8 dried red chillies, seeds removed
1½ teaspoons coriander seeds
½ teaspoon cumin seeds
1 cardamom pod
1 teaspoon sea salt flakes
2 teaspoons chopped fresh galangal root (peel it first)
2 lemongrass stems, lower one-third only, chopped
3 kaffir lime leaves, chopped
1 tablespoon chopped coriander (cilantro) root (washed well before chopping)
1 red Asian shallot, finely chopped
3 garlic cloves, crushed
1 teaspoon fermented shrimp paste; if unavailable, use 1 tablespoon fish sauce

Duck & Pork Sausage Cassoulet

SERVES 8

Place the beans in a large saucepan and cover with 3 litres (101 fl oz/ 12 cups) cold water. Bring to the boil over high heat, then cook for 15 minutes. Remove from the heat and leave the beans to soak for 2 hours in the cooking liquid.

Preheat the oven to 120°C/250°F (fan-forced). Heat a large flameproof casserole dish over medium heat. Add the olive oil and pork belly cubes. Cook, turning frequently, until the pork is golden and most of the fat has been released. Remove the pork to a bowl and set aside.

Place the duck, skin side down, in the hot casserole dish. Cook for 5 minutes before turning, to achieve a rich, dark crust on the skin. Cook the other side until browned, then remove and leave to rest with the pork.

Brown the sausages in the same dish, turning occasionally, then add to the bowl with the pork and duck. Add the onion, garlic, carrot and celery to the casserole dish. Reduce the heat slightly and cook for 10 minutes, or until the onion is very soft, stirring occasionally to cook evenly. Stir in the thyme sprigs, bay leaves, salt, passata and a generous grind of black pepper.

Return the cooked pork cubes, duck and sausages to the casserole. Drain the beans, then add them to the dish, along with 1.25 litres (42 fl oz/5 cups) water. Transfer the casserole dish to the oven and cook for 3 hours. At this point, a light crust should be forming. Pierce the crust slightly with a fork in about seven places. If the beans are looking dry, add a little extra water down the side of the dish.

Return to the oven and bake for 1– 1½ hours. The cassoulet is ready when a rich, dark crust has formed, the beans are cooked, the mixture looks a little saucy, and the duck is tender and falling from the bone.

Serve in deep bowls, with a green salad and fresh crusty bread.

350 g (12½ oz/1¾ cups) dried cannellini beans
1 tablespoon olive oil
200 g (7 oz) piece of pork belly, cut into 2 cm (¾ inch) cubes, leaving the skin on
4 duck leg quarters
4 fresh garlic pork sausages
1 large onion, finely chopped
3 garlic cloves, crushed
1 carrot, cut in half lengthways
2 celery stalks
2 thyme sprigs
2 bay leaves
2 teaspoons sea salt flakes
125 ml (4 fl oz/½ cup) tomato passata
fresh green salad, to serve
crusty bread, to serve

Creamy Calvados Chicken

SERVES 4

Heat the olive oil and butter in a large heavy-based saucepan over medium heat. Add the shallot and bacon and cook for 5 minutes, or until the shallot has softened and the bacon is beginning to crisp.

Add the chicken and cook for 2–3 minutes on each side. Add the Calvados and stir to deglaze the pan.

Stir in the cider, lemon thyme sprigs, apple wedges, salt and pepper. Cover and cook over low heat for 45 minutes, or until the chicken is cooked through and tender. Check the pan occasionally, adding a tablespoon or two of water if it becomes dry.

Gently stir in the crème fraîche. Allow to simmer for a further minute, then remove from the heat.

Sprinkle with the parsley and serve with steamed potatoes and a fresh green salad.

Calvados is an apple brandy from the Normandy region in northern France. If you don't have any, simply leave it out, or use Armagnac or brandy instead.

1 tablespoon olive oil
2 teaspoons butter
2 French shallots, finely chopped
1 streaky bacon slice, finely chopped
4 free-range chicken drumsticks
4 free-range chicken thigh cutlets, bone in
2 tablespoons Calvados (see tip)
125 ml (4 fl oz/½ cup) apple cider
3 lemon thyme sprigs
2 pink eating apples, cored and cut into 6 wedges each
1 teaspoon sea salt flakes
¼ teaspoon freshly ground black pepper
80 g (2¾ oz/⅓ cup) crème fraîche, light sour cream or pouring (single/ light) cream
3 tablespoons finely chopped flat-leaf (Italian) parsley
steamed new potatoes, to serve
green salad, to serve

Slow-Cooked Chicken Enchiladas

SERVES 4–6

Heat the stock and garlic in a saucepan over medium heat until almost boiling. Add the chicken and cover the pan, then reduce the heat to low and simmer for 1 hour. Transfer the chicken to a bowl and set aside.

Add the tomatillos and jalapeño chillies to the stock. Bring back to a simmer and cook for 15 minutes, or until the chillies are tender. Allow to cool a little, then strain the mixture through a sieve, into a bowl, retaining the stock.

Meanwhile, preheat the oven to 160°C/320°F (fan-forced). Place the tomatillos, jalapeño chillies and garlic cloves in a blender. Add the onion and salt and process until a rough sauce forms. Add 170 ml (5½ fl oz/⅔ cup) of the reserved stock and process until well blended.

Shred the chicken finely. Place in a bowl and add 250 ml (8½ fl oz/ 1 cup) of the tomatillo sauce, stirring to coat the chicken in the sauce.

Lay the tortillas on a clean board. Place the chicken mixture along the centre of each tortilla, dividing it evenly. Roll the tortilla sides up and over to enclose the filling, then lay the enchiladas in a baking dish. Pour the remaining tomatillo sauce over the top. Spoon the crema down the centre, then sprinkle with the cheese. Bake for 20–25 minutes, or until completely heated through.

Meanwhile, combine the salsa ingredients together in a small bowl. Serve the enchiladas straight from the oven, with the salsa.

Mexican crema is a cultured cream used widely in that cuisine. It can be made in batches and stored in the fridge for 2 weeks. To make crema for this recipe, blend 60 ml (2 fl oz/¼ cup) buttermilk, yoghurt or sour cream with 125 ml (4 fl oz/½ cup) thick (double/heavy) cream and a pinch of sea salt. Cover and store at room temperature for 6–8 hours, or overnight. The crema can then be refrigerated until needed. Serve at room temperature.

500 ml (17 fl oz/2 cups) chicken stock
2 garlic cloves, smashed
500 g (1 lb 2 oz) boneless, skinless chicken thighs
800 g (1 lb 12 oz) tinned tomatillos, drained
2 jalapeño chillies, stems removed
1 small white onion, chopped
1 teaspoon sea salt flakes
8 large corn tortillas
185 ml (6½ fl oz/¾ cup) Mexican crema (see tip) or light sour cream
25 g (1 oz/¼ cup) grated Manchego or parmesan

FRESH SALSA
1 small white onion, finely chopped
1 jalapeño chilli, seeds removed, finely chopped
25 g (1 oz/½ cup) finely chopped coriander (cilantro) leaves

Butter Chicken

Combine the yoghurt, lemon juice and garam masala in a bowl. Add the chicken and mix until well coated. Cover and refrigerate for 6 hours or overnight.

Heat the vegetable oil in a large saucepan over medium heat. Add the garlic, ginger, chillies, cinnamon stick, salt, coriander, cumin and turmeric. Cook, stirring, for 1 minute, or until fragrant. Add the chicken and cook for 3–4 minutes, stirring well to coat it in the spices.

Stir in the passata, sugar and almond meal, then cover and simmer over low heat for 20 minutes.

Stir in the cream, then remove from the heat.

Serve with basmati rice, garnished with coriander.

SERVES 4

125 g (4½ oz/½ cup) plain yoghurt
1 tablespoon lemon juice
2 teaspoons garam masala
500 g (1 lb 2 oz) boneless, skinless
  chicken thighs, cut into 3 cm
  (1¼ inch) chunks
1 tablespoon vegetable oil
2 garlic cloves, crushed
3 cm (1¼ inch) piece of fresh ginger,
  peeled and grated
2 small dried chillies
1 cinnamon stick
1 teaspoon sea salt flakes
1 teaspoon ground coriander
1 teaspoon ground cumin
¼ teaspoon ground turmeric
185 ml (6½ fl oz/¾ cup) tomato
  passata
1 teaspoon sugar
1½ tablespoons almond meal
185 ml (6½ fl oz/¾ cup) pouring
  (single/light) cream
steamed basmati rice, to serve
coriander (cilantro) leaves, to garnish

Duck Ragu with Pasta

SERVES 4–6

Heat a large heavy-based saucepan over medium–high heat. Season the duck with sea salt flakes and freshly ground black pepper. Add the duck to the pan, skin side down, and brown for 10 minutes, turning once during cooking. Remove to a plate.

Discard any excess fat from the pan, leaving about 2 teaspoons. Add the olive oil and cook the leek, garlic, carrot and celery over low heat for 5 minutes. Add the herbs and fennel seeds and cook for a further minute. Return the duck to the pan.

Pour in the verjuice, allow to bubble for a minute or two, then add the orange zest and juice, stock and a few shakes of chilli flakes, if using. Bring to the boil, cover the pan, reduce the heat to a low simmer and cook slowly for 1½ hours.

Remove the lid and simmer on low heat for a further 20 minutes, or until the liquid has reduced to a brothy consistency. Remove the duck legs, pull the meat from the bones and return it to the ragu; discard the skin and bones. Discard the thyme sprigs, rosemary and bay leaves. Season to taste with salt and black pepper.

Meanwhile, bring a large saucepan of water to the boil and cook the pasta for 10 minutes, or until 'al dente'. Drain and toss with the ragu and parsley.

Verjuice is made from the juice of unfermented grapes. It adds a gentle acidic flavour to dishes.

4 duck leg quarters, trimmed of excess fat
2 tablespoons olive oil
2 leeks, white part only, cut in half lengthways, then chopped
3 garlic cloves, finely chopped
2 carrots, halved lengthways, then chopped
2 celery stalks, sliced
2 large thyme sprigs
2 rosemary sprigs
2 bay leaves
1 teaspoon fennel seeds, crushed with a knife
375 ml (12½ fl oz/1½ cups) verjuice (see tip) or white wine
zest and juice of 1 orange
500 ml (17 fl oz/2 cups) chicken stock
chilli flakes (optional)
350 g (12½ oz) short pasta, such as orecchiette
2 generous tablespoons chopped flat-leaf (Italian) parsley

Chunky Chicken Pot Pies

MAKES 4

To make the pastry, roughly rub the butter cubes into the flour and salt, without overworking — there should still be small lumps of butter. Make a well in the centre. Gradually add the cold water, mixing it in with your hands to form a dough. Shape the dough into a disc, wrap in plastic wrap and rest in the fridge for 30 minutes.

On a floured surface, roll the dough out into a rectangle 1.5 cm (½ inch) thick. Fold one of the short ends of the dough two-thirds of the way into the centre. Fold the remaining pastry third back over to the opposite end, to form a book shape. Wrap and chill again for 25 minutes. Repeat this folding process twice more. After the final folding, ensure the pastry has rested in the fridge for at least 30 minutes before using.

Meanwhile make the filling. Heat the oil in a saucepan and brown the chicken over high heat for 8–10 minutes. Add the leek, carrot, celery and garlic and cook over medium heat for 5 minutes, or until the vegetables soften. Add the thyme and bay leaf and season with salt and pepper. Stir in the wine and cook for 2–3 minutes, or until reduced by half, then add the stock. Cover and leave to cook over low heat for 45 minutes.

Remove the lid from the pan. Stir in the cream and simmer gently for a further 25 minutes. Remove and discard the thyme and bay leaf. Stir in the mustard and tarragon, then stir the spinach through until wilted. Remove from the heat and leave to cool.

Preheat the oven to 180°C/350°F (fan-forced). Roll the pastry out to 1 cm (½ inch) thick. Divide the chicken mixture among four 250 ml (8½ fl oz/1 cup) ramekins. Brush around the rim with beaten egg, so the pastry will adhere. Place a ramekin on the pastry and cut out a circle a bit larger than the ramekin. Place the pastry over the filling, pressing the dough down around the outside of the ramekin. Repeat with the remaining pastry, until all the pies are topped. Using a knife, make a small slit in the centre of each pie lid, to allow steam to escape.

Bake for 30 minutes, or until the pastry is golden and puffed. Serve hot, with salad or vegetables.

ROUGH PUFF PASTRY
225 g (8 oz/1½ cups) plain (all-purpose) flour, plus extra for dusting
½ teaspoon sea salt flakes
225 g (8 oz) cold butter, cut into small cubes
80 ml (2½ fl oz/⅓ cup) cold water, mixed with a squeeze of lemon
1 egg, beaten

FILLING
1 tablespoon olive oil
700 g (1 lb 9 oz) skinless chicken thigh fillets, trimmed and cut into 2.5–3 cm (1–1¼ inch) chunks
2 leeks, white part only, cut in half lengthways, then chopped
1 medium–large carrot, chopped
1 celery stalk, chopped
1 large garlic clove, finely chopped
3 lemon thyme or thyme sprigs
1 bay leaf
125 ml (4 fl oz/½ cup) dry white wine
250 ml (8½ fl oz/1 cup) chicken stock
185 ml (6½ fl oz/¾ cup) thickened (whipping) cream
1 teaspoon dijon mustard
1 tablespoon chopped tarragon or sage
50 g (1¾ oz) spinach, thickly shredded

Chicken Cacciatore

Heat a large heavy-based or cast-iron saucepan over high heat. Brown the chicken on both sides for 3–4 minutes (you won't need any oil in the pan at this stage, as there is plenty of fat in the skin). Remove the chicken to a plate.

Add the pancetta to the pan and cook, stirring, over high heat for 2 minutes.

Reduce the heat to medium. Add the olive oil, onion, garlic and mushrooms and sauté for 5 minutes, or until the onion has softened and the mushrooms have coloured. Add the capsicum and cook for 2 minutes, until softened. Now add the bay leaves and thyme sprigs, and return the chicken to the pan.

Pour in the wine, then allow to bubble for 3–4 minutes to reduce slightly. Stir in the tomatoes and stock, then cover and simmer over low heat for 1 hour.

Remove the lid and simmer for a further 5 minutes, or until the sauce has reduced slightly. Stir in the olives and sugar, then season to taste with sea salt flakes and freshly ground black pepper.

Garnish with parsley and serve with your choice of accompaniment.

SERVES 4

4 free-range chicken leg quarters, or 4 chicken drumsticks and 4 thigh cutlets, skin on
100 g (3½ oz) pancetta, chopped
2 tablespoons olive oil
1 large onion, finely chopped
2 large garlic cloves, finely chopped
200 g (7 oz) Swiss brown or button mushrooms, quartered
1 red capsicum (bell pepper), thinly sliced
2 bay leaves
2 thyme sprigs
185 ml (6½ fl oz/¾ cup) white or red wine
400 g (14 oz) tinned cherry tomatoes or crushed tomatoes
250 ml (8½ fl oz/1 cup) chicken stock
12 pitted kalamata olives
½ teaspoon sugar
chopped flat-leaf (Italian) parsley or basil, to serve
crusty bread, crunchy roasted potatoes or mashed potato, to serve

Baked Tarragon Chicken

SERVES 4

Preheat the oven to 140°C/275°F (fan-forced).

Place the chicken pieces in a large baking dish and season with sea salt flakes and freshly ground black pepper. Brush with the melted butter, then sprinkle with the tarragon. Tuck the lemon quarters in and around the chicken.

Cover the baking dish tightly with foil, transfer to the oven and bake for 1½ hours.

Remove the foil and add the potatoes to the dish. Brush the chicken and potatoes with the cooking juices from the bottom of the dish.

Return to the oven, leaving the foil off, and bake for a further 1 hour.

Increase the oven temperature to 180°C/350°F (fan-forced). Bake for a final 20 minutes, or until the potatoes are cooked through and the chicken skin is golden.

Serve the chicken and potatoes with a green salad.

4 free-range chicken leg quarters
1½ tablespoons melted butter
3 tablespoons tarragon leaves, or
  1 tablespoon dried tarragon
2 lemons, quartered
2 large potatoes, peeled and quartered
green salad, to serve

PORK

Slow-Cooked Pork Lasagne

SERVES 8

Heat the olive oil in a large heavy-based saucepan over medium heat. Add the onion, carrot and celery. Cover and cook for 15 minutes, stirring occasionally, and adding a tablespoon of water if the vegetables catch on the base of the pan. Add the garlic, bay leaf, rosemary, salt and pepper and stir until the garlic is fragrant.

Stir in the vinegar and wine. When the wine is simmering, add the pork and cook for 3 minutes on each side.

Add the tomatoes and passata, stir and cover the pan. Cook over low heat for 2½ hours, stirring occasionally, and adding a little water if the sauce becomes dry.

Preheat the oven to 160°C/320°F (fan-forced).

Remove the pork from the pan. Finely shred the pork using two forks, then stir the shredded pork back into the sauce.

Pour about 375 ml (12½ fl oz/1½ cups) of the sauce into a large baking dish. Then layer the lasagne sheets and sauce into the dish, finishing with the sauce.

In a small bowl, blend the crème fraîche with 2 tablespoons water. Spoon the crème fraîche over the top of the dish and scatter with the cheese.

Bake for 50 minutes, or until the topping is golden brown. Allow to stand for 10 minutes before serving. Serve hot, with a green salad.

In this recipe, crème fraîche is used as a substitute for the more conventional béchamel sauce. You can make your own crème fraîche at home by blending 60 ml (2 fl oz/¼ cup) buttermilk with 340 ml (11½ fl oz/1⅓ cups) thick (double/heavy) cream, and leaving overnight at room temperature before using.

2 tablespoons olive oil
1 large onion, finely chopped
1 large carrot, finely chopped
2 celery stalks, finely chopped
2 garlic cloves, crushed
1 bay leaf
2 rosemary sprigs
2 teaspoons sea salt flakes
1 teaspoon freshly ground black pepper
1 tablespoon balsamic vinegar
125 ml (4 fl oz/½ cup) shiraz or dry red wine
1 kg (2 lb 3 oz) skinless pork belly
400 g (14 oz) tinned crushed tomatoes
500 ml (17 fl oz/2 cups) tomato passata
300 g (10½ oz) fresh lasagne sheets
375 g (13 fl oz/1½ cups) crème fraîche (see tip)
60 g (2 oz/½ cup) grated romano cheese
green salad, to serve

Ecuadorian Slow-Roasted Pork with Agrio Sauce & Salad

SERVES 12

In a bowl, combine the lime juice, grapefruit juice, olive oil, garlic, cumin, oregano, salt and pepper. Rub the mixture over the pork leg, working it into the meat, and into the scored lines in the skin. Cover the pork loosely with a cloth, allowing air to circulate, and rest the pork overnight in the fridge. Remove from the fridge an hour before cooking.

Preheat the oven to 150°C/300°F (fan-forced).

Spread the onion slices in a deep baking dish, and place a rack in the dish. Lay the pork leg on the rack. Pour the beer into the baking dish. Cover the dish loosely with foil, transfer to the oven and bake for 4 hours.

Remove the foil, add the potatoes to the pan and increase the oven temperature to 180°C/350°F (fan-forced). Roast for 1¼ hours, or until the potatoes are tender, and the pork skin is crisp. Remove from the oven and allow to rest for 10 minutes.

Meanwhile, combine the agrio sauce ingredients in a bowl and allow to stand at room temperature for 30 minutes before serving.

To make the salad, combine the cabbage, mint and coriander in a large bowl. Dress with the salt, lime juice and olive oil and toss well.

Serve the rested pork with the potatoes, agrio sauce and salad.

juice of 2 limes
juice of 1 grapefruit
60 ml (2 fl oz/¼ cup) olive oil
15 garlic cloves, crushed
1 tablespoon ground cumin
1 tablespoon dried oregano
2 teaspoons sea salt flakes
1 teaspoon freshly ground black pepper
3 kg (6 lb 10 oz) pork leg, skin scored (ask your butcher)
2 onions, sliced
500 ml (17 fl oz/2 cups) beer
12 small whole potatoes, scrubbed

AGRIO SAUCE
1 small tomato, finely chopped
1 small red onion, finely chopped
1 long red chilli, finely sliced
25 g (1 oz/½ cup) chopped coriander (cilantro) leaves
2 tablespoons grapefruit juice
2 tablespoons orange juice
1 tablespoon lime juice
1 tablespoon lemon juice
1 teaspoon soft brown sugar
½ teaspoon sea salt flakes

SALAD
1 small green cabbage, shredded
50 g (1¾ oz/1 cup, firmly packed) finely chopped mint leaves
50 g (1¾ oz/1 cup) chopped coriander (cilantro) leaves
½ teaspoon sea salt flakes
juice of 1 lime
1 tablespoon olive oil

Smoky Chipotle Barbecued Pork Ribs

Preheat the oven to 150°C/300°F (fan-forced).

Combine the dry rub ingredients in a small bowl. Sprinkle evenly over both sides of the pork ribs, pressing it in well.

Wrap the ribs in foil, then place in a single layer on a large baking tray. Transfer to the oven and bake for 2½ hours.

Remove the foil-wrapped ribs from the oven and leave until cool enough to handle.

To make the sauce, heat the olive oil in a small saucepan over low heat and cook the garlic and apple for about 4 minutes, or until soft. Stir in the salt, paprika, chillies, passata, maple syrup and vinegar. Continue to cook over low heat, stirring occasionally, for about 10 minutes, or until the mixture is thick and saucy. Set aside.

Preheat a barbecue grill to medium heat.

Unwrap the ribs, and brush the sauce over both sides. Grill the ribs on both sides, until charred.

Transfer the ribs to a chopping board. Use a sharp knife to cut between the bones.

Pile the ribs onto a serving platter and serve with potato salad and green salad.

4 racks pork baby back ribs, each cut in half for easier handling
potato salad, to serve
green salad, to serve

DRY RUB
3 teaspoons sea salt flakes
3 teaspoons smoked paprika
2 teaspoons soft brown sugar
2 teaspoons dried oregano
1½ teaspoons freshly ground black pepper

SAUCE
1 tablespoon olive oil
2 garlic cloves, crushed
2 cooking apples, peeled, cored and grated
1 teaspoon sea salt
1 teaspoon sweet paprika
2 chipotle chillies in adobo sauce, chopped
250 ml (8½ fl oz/1 cup) tomato passata
60 ml (2 fl oz/¼ cup) maple syrup
2 tablespoons cider vinegar

Hungarian Pork & Beef Goulash

SERVES 6

Heat the olive oil in a large heavy-based saucepan over medium heat. Add the onion and cook, stirring, for 10–12 minutes, or until the onion is soft and beginning to turn an even golden colour.

Add the capsicums and tomato and cook, stirring, for a further 2–3 minutes. Stir in the hot paprika and salt, then add the beef and stir to coat with the onion. Cook, stirring, for a few minutes to seal the beef pieces. Now add the pork and cook, stirring, for a further 5 minutes.

Stir in the sweet paprika and 500 ml (17 fl oz/2 cups) boiling water. Cover the pan, reduce the heat to low and simmer, stirring occasionally, for 1 hour.

Add the potato pieces to the pan, pushing them down into the sauce. The liquid should be thickening, but still be saucy; if it is looking a little dry, add another 250 ml (8½ fl oz/1 cup) water. Replace the lid and cook on low for a further 40 minutes.

Serve the goulash in deep bowls, with fresh sourdough bread and green salad.

60 ml (2 fl oz/¼ cup) olive oil
3 onions, chopped
1 red capsicum (bell pepper), finely chopped
1 green capsicum (bell pepper), finely chopped
1 large tomato, chopped
1 tablespoon hot paprika
2 teaspoons sea salt flakes
400 g (14 oz) stewing beef, cut into 3 cm (1¼ inch) chunks
600 g (1 lb 5 oz) pork shoulder, cut into 3 cm (1¼ inch) chunks
25 g (1 oz/¼ cup) sweet paprika
4 potatoes, peeled and cut lengthways into quarters
sourdough bread, to serve
green salad, to serve

Slow-Cooked Pork Ragu with Rigatoni

SERVES 6

Heat the olive oil in a large heavy-based saucepan over medium heat. Add the onion. Cover and cook, stirring occasionally, for 15 minutes, or until very soft and slightly golden; if the onion browns too quickly, add a tablespoon of water.

Add the garlic, chilli flakes and salt and cook, stirring, for 1 minute. Add the wine, dried basil, bay leaves and sugar. When the wine is hot, add the pork. Allow the pork to seal for 1 minute, then turn and cook the other side.

Stir in the tomatoes and passata, and 250 ml (8½ fl oz/1 cup) water. Cover the pan and reduce the heat to low. Cook for 3 hours, checking every 30 minutes to stir and add more water if needed. The sauce should be fairly wet during cooking, but after 3 hours it should have reduced, and become thick and syrupy.

Shred the pork in the pan using two forks. Stir the basil leaves through, to coat them in the sauce.

Fill a large saucepan with water and add 2 teaspoons salt. Bring to the boil, add the pasta and cook for 10 minutes, or until al dente. Drain the pasta and return to the pot. Add a ladleful of sauce to the pasta and stir it through.

Serve the pasta with the pork ragu, parmesan and a green salad.

2 tablespoons olive oil
2 red onions, finely chopped
2 garlic cloves, crushed
1 teaspoon chilli flakes
1½ teaspoons sea salt flakes
185 ml (6½ fl oz/¾ cup) dry white wine
2 teaspoons dried basil
2 bay leaves
½ teaspoon soft brown sugar
500 g (1 lb 2 oz) skinless pork belly slices
400 g (14 oz) tinned crushed tomatoes
500 ml (17 fl oz/2 cups) tomato passata
50 g (1¾ oz/1 cup, firmly packed) whole basil leaves, plus extra to garnish
500 g (1 lb 2 oz) rigatoni
shaved parmesan, to serve
green salad, to serve

Slow-Roasted Pork Shoulder with Root Vegetables & Apple Jus

SERVES 6

Preheat the oven to 130°C/265°F (fan-forced).

In a small bowl, combine the salt, pepper, sugar and lemon juice. Place the pork, skin side down, on a clean board. Rub the seasoning mixture into the meat, taking care to keep the skin clean and dry.

Arrange the apple and onion slices in a baking dish as a base for the pork to rest on. Add the rosemary sprigs and place the pork on top.

Roast for 1 hour to allow the skin to dry out, then cover the dish loosely with foil, reduce the oven temperature to 110°C/230°F (fan-forced) and roast for a further 4 hours.

Remove the baking dish from the oven and remove the foil. Place the vegetables around and under the pork. Baste the vegetables and the meaty sides of the pork with the cooking juices and sprinkle the vegetables and the pork skin with sea salt. Pierce the pork skin with a bamboo skewer in many places.

Increase the oven temperature to 180°C/350°F (fan-forced). Return the dish to the oven to roast, uncovered, for a further 1 hour, or until the vegetables are cooked, the pork is very tender and the pork skin is puffed and crackling.

Transfer the pork, carrots, parsnips and turnips to a warm serving dish.

To make the apple jus, use a spatula to scrape the pan juices, apple and onion fragments from the baking dish into a narrow jug. Scoop the fat off the top, then use a stick mixer to blend the jus.

Transfer the apple jus to a serving jug and serve alongside the roasted pork and vegetables.

1 teaspoon sea salt flakes, plus extra for seasoning
½ teaspoon freshly ground black pepper
½ teaspoon soft brown sugar
1 tablespoon lemon juice
2.5 kg (5½ lb) pork shoulder, bone in, skin scored
2 apples, cored and sliced into rings
1 red onion, sliced
3 rosemary sprigs
12 baby carrots, scrubbed, leaves trimmed
3 parsnips, peeled and cut in half lengthways
3 turnips, peeled and cut into quarters

Pulled Pork Tacos with Fresh Pineapple Salsa

SERVES 8

Preheat the oven to 130°C/265°F (fan-forced).

Put the olive oil in a small bowl. Add the cumin, paprika, oregano, chilli, salt, garlic and vinegar and mix to a paste. Spread the paste over the pork.

Place the pork in a baking dish or casserole dish in which it fits snugly. Tuck the lime slices, orange slices and onion wedges around and over the pork. Cover the dish with baking paper, then a sheet of foil, creating a tight seal.

Transfer to the oven and bake for 5 hours. Remove the pork from oven and unwrap. Leave until cool enough to handle.

Near serving time, combine the pineapple salsa ingredients in a mixing bowl.

To toast the tortillas, heat a small dry frying pan over high heat. Toast each tortilla for 5–10 seconds on one side only, then wrap in a cloth to keep warm and soft.

Remove the bone from the pork — it should pull out easily. Using tongs, break the meat into large chunks. Heat a large frying pan over high heat and add an extra 2 tablespoons olive oil. Working in batches, taking care not to overcrowd the pan, sear the pork chunks all over, using the tongs to tear the chunks into smaller pieces as they char slightly. Repeat with the remaining pork.

Serve the pork with the pineapple salsa, warm tortillas, lettuce, and lime wedges for squeezing over.

2 tablespoons olive oil, plus extra for charring the pork
1 tablespoon ground cumin
1 tablespoon smoked paprika
2 teaspoons dried oregano
2 teaspoons chilli flakes
2 teaspoons sea salt flakes
3 garlic cloves, crushed
1 tablespoon cider vinegar
3 kg (6 lb 10 oz) pork shoulder, bone in
1 lime, skin on, thickly sliced
1 orange, skin on, thickly sliced
1 red onion, cut into thin wedges

PINEAPPLE SALSA
190 g (6½ oz/1 cup) finely diced fresh pineapple
pinch of sea salt flakes
1 red onion, finely chopped
25 g (1 oz/½ cup) chopped coriander (cilantro) leaves

TO SERVE
corn tortillas
baby cos (romaine) lettuce leaves
2 limes, cut into wedges

Asian-Style Caramel Pork

Heat 2 teaspoons of the oil in a wok until hot. In three batches, brown the pork over high heat, removing each batch to a plate. Drain the pork fat from the wok.

Add the remaining oil to the wok, along with the chilli, shallot, garlic and the coriander stalks. Cook over medium heat for 2 minutes.

Return the pork to the wok. Stir in the soy sauce, sugar, star anise and cinnamon stick and 375 ml (12½ fl oz/1½ cups) water. Reduce the heat to low, cover with a lid and leave to simmer for 1½ hours.

Remove the lid and simmer over low heat for 10 minutes, or until the sauce is syrupy. Stir in the fish sauce.

Garnish with the coriander leaves. Serve with steamed rice and greens, with lime wedges for squeezing over.

Leave the seeds in the chillies if you like more heat.

SERVES 4

1½ tablespoons sunflower, rice bran or vegetable oil

1 kg (2 lb 3 oz) pork belly or pork slices, cut into 3 cm (1¼ inch) pieces

2 bird's eye chillies, seeds removed (see tip), finely chopped

6 French shallots, chopped

3 garlic cloves, finely chopped

50 g (1¾ oz/1 bunch) coriander (cilantro), stalks finely chopped, leaves reserved for garnishing

80 ml (2½ fl oz/⅓ cup) light soy sauce

180 g (6½ oz/1 cup) shaved palm sugar (jaggery)

1 star anise

1 cinnamon stick

2 tablespoons fish sauce

steamed white rice, to serve

steamed greens, to serve

lime wedges (optional), to serve

Braised Pork Shoulder with Apple Cider & Red Cabbage

SERVES 6–8

Preheat the oven to 140°C/275°F (fan-forced).

Season the pork generously with sea salt flakes and freshly ground black pepper. Heat a large flameproof casserole dish over high heat. Add the olive oil and brown the pork well on all sides; this will take 10–15 minutes. Remove the pork from the dish, reduce the heat to medium and cook the bacon until crispy.

Add the onion to the dish and cook, stirring, for 6–8 minutes, or until softened. Add the garlic and cook for 1 minute, until fragrant. Return the pork to the dish and pour over the cider. Add the crushed juniper berries.

Cover the pork with baking paper to reduce evaporation, then put the lid on. Transfer to the oven and bake for 2 hours.

Remove the dish from the oven. Carefully turn the pork over, then place the cabbage around the side of the dish. Pour the vinegar over the cabbage, replace the baking paper and lid, and return to the oven for 1 hour, or until the pork is falling-apart tender.

Using tongs, break the pork into large chunks and remove the bone.

Serve the braised pork and cabbage with mashed potato, with the pan juices spooned over.

1 kg (2 lb 3 oz) pork shoulder, bone in
1 tablespoon olive oil
150 g (5½ oz) thickly cut smoked streaky bacon, cut into 1 cm (½ inch) pieces
2 onions, thinly sliced
2 garlic cloves, crushed
375 ml (12½ fl oz/1½ cups) apple cider
10 juniper berries, crushed
1 small red cabbage, about 1 kg (2 lb 3 oz), shredded
60 ml (2 fl oz/¼ cup) cider vinegar
mashed potato, to serve

BEEF

Slow-Cooked Beef Stroganoff

SERVES 6

Preheat the oven to 130°C/265°F (fan-forced).

Heat 2 tablespoons of the olive oil in a large frying pan over high heat. Brown the beef well on all sides for about 10 minutes, then remove the beef to a casserole dish.

Reduce the heat under the frying pan to medium. Add the onion and cook for 6–8 minutes, or until softened. Add the garlic, salt, pepper and passata and cook, stirring, for another minute. Add the vodka and stock and stir to deglaze the pan. Pour the onion mixture over the beef.

Cover the casserole dish tightly with baking paper, then a sheet of foil, to reduce evaporation. Transfer to the oven and cook for 3 hours, or until the beef is very tender when tested with a fork.

Remove the beef from the casserole and shred roughly using two forks. Return the shredded beef to the casserole dish.

Heat a frying pan over medium heat and add the butter and 2 teaspoons olive oil. When the butter foams, add the mushrooms and cook, stirring occasionally, for about 5 minutes. Remove from the heat, stir in the crème fraîche, then add the mushroom mixture to the casserole and stir it through.

Place the baking paper and foil back on the casserole dish, sealing it tightly. Return to the oven for a further 30 minutes to heat through.

Serve garnished with the parsley, with dill pickles and boiled potatoes.

2 tablespoons olive oil, plus an extra 2 teaspoons
1 kg (2 lb 3 oz) piece of stewing steak
1 onion, thinly sliced
2 garlic cloves, crushed
1 teaspoon sea salt flakes
½ teaspoon freshly ground black pepper
125 ml (4 fl oz/½ cup) tomato passata
2 tablespoons vodka
250 ml (8½ fl oz/1 cup) beef stock
2 tablespoons butter
500 g (1 lb 2 oz) button mushrooms, sliced
125 g (4½ oz/½ cup) crème fraîche or sour cream
3 tablespoons finely chopped flat-leaf (Italian) parsley
dill pickles, to serve
boiled new potatoes, to serve

Sticky Oxtail Stew
with Creamy Polenta

SERVES 4

Preheat the oven to 130°C/265°F (fan-forced).

Season the oxtail pieces generously with sea salt flakes and freshly ground black pepper. Place the flour in a bowl and coat each piece in the flour, shaking off the excess.

In a large flameproof casserole dish, heat the olive oil over medium–high heat. Working in batches, add the oxtail pieces and brown all over; you may need to add a little extra oil. Remove the oxtail to a plate.

Add the celery, carrot and garlic to the pan, along with the tomatoes, stock, wine, bay leaves and rosemary sprig. Cover with a sheet of baking paper and the lid, then transfer to the oven and bake for 2 hours.

Turn the oxtail pieces over, submerging them in the sauce. Replace the baking paper and lid and return to the oven for a further 3 hours.

Remove from the oven and leave until cool enough to handle. Remove the oxtail pieces from the sauce, then remove the meat from the bones. Discard the bones. Skim the fat from the surface of the sauce and return the meat to the pan.

To make the polenta, bring 1 litre (34 fl oz/4 cups) water to the boil in a saucepan over medium–high heat. Add the salt. While stirring gently, pour the polenta into the boiling water in a steady stream. Continue stirring as the polenta thickens. Reduce the heat to low and continue stirring, then cover with a lid and continue cooking for 30 minutes, stirring vigorously every 10 minutes or so, scraping down the sides, bottom and into the corner of the pan. Stir in the butter, then cover and allow to rest for 10 minutes before serving.

Spoon the polenta into deep bowls. Spoon the oxtail stew over, garnish with the parsley and serve.

1.3 kg (2 lb 14 oz) oxtail, segmented between the bones (your butcher will do this for you)
35 g (1¼ oz/¼ cup) plain (all-purpose) flour
2 tablespoons olive oil, approximately
2 celery stalks, thickly sliced
4 carrots, cut into large chunks
2 garlic cloves, crushed
400 g (14 oz) tinned crushed tomatoes
500 ml (17 fl oz/2 cups) beef stock
125 ml (4 fl oz/½ cup) shiraz or dry red wine
2 bay leaves
1 rosemary sprig
15 g (½ oz/½ cup) finely chopped flat-leaf (Italian) parsley

CREAMY POLENTA
1 teaspoon sea salt
150 g (5½ oz/1 cup) polenta
2 tablespoons butter

Beef Rendang

SERVES 4

Place all the spice paste ingredients in a small food processor. Blend to a chunky paste.

Heat the peanut oil in a large heavy-based saucepan over high heat. Working in three batches, brown the beef well, removing each batch to a plate.

Add the spice paste to the pan and cook, stirring, for 2 minutes. Return the beef to the pan.

In a separate frying pan, lightly toast the coconut for 2 minutes, or until pale golden.

Add the toasted coconut to the beef, along with the lemongrass, lime leaves, cinnamon sticks, sugar and salt. Stir in the coconut milk and 500 ml (17 fl oz/2 cups) water.

Put the lid on and bring to a simmer, then reduce the heat to low. Cook, covered, at a slow simmer for 2½ hours.

Remove the lid. Simmer, uncovered, over low heat for a further 20–30 minutes, or until the curry is quite dry.

Serve with steamed rice and steamed greens, if desired.

2 tablespoons peanut or vegetable oil
1 kg (2 lb 3 oz) trimmed stewing
  steak, cut into 3 cm (1¼ inch) cubes
25 g (1 oz/¼ cup) desiccated
  (shredded) coconut
1 lemongrass stem, white part only,
  bruised
6 kaffir lime leaves
2 cinnamon sticks
1 tablespoon sugar
1 teaspoon sea salt flakes
400 ml (14 fl oz) tinned coconut milk
steamed white rice, to serve
steamed greens, to serve (optional)

SPICE PASTE
6 French shallots, peeled
4 large garlic cloves, peeled
2 lemongrass stems, white part only,
  chopped
6 bird's eye chillies, seeds removed
  from 3 of the chillies
1½ tablespoons finely chopped peeled
  fresh ginger
1½ tablespoons finely chopped peeled
  fresh galangal
1 teaspoon ground coriander
1 teaspoon ground turmeric
2 tablespoons peanut or vegetable oil

Slow-Cooked Cuban Beef

Season the beef well with sea salt flakes and freshly ground black pepper. Heat 2 tablespoons olive oil in a large heavy-based saucepan over high heat. Add the beef in a single layer, working in two batches if necessary. Cook for 4 minutes to brown well, then turn and cook for a few minutes to brown the other side. Remove from the pan and set aside.

Add the onion, carrot, celery, garlic and bay leaf to the pan. Cook for 4–5 minutes, then add the tomatoes, vinegar and stock. Stir to scrape the base of the pan, then add the beef back in.

Put the lid on the pan, reduce the heat to low and simmer gently for 2 hours, checking to stir occasionally and top up the liquid with water if necessary.

Heat another 1 tablespoon olive oil in a large frying pan over medium heat. Add the capsicums and cook, tossing occasionally, for 5 minutes, or until softened. Stir in the tomato paste and fry for a couple of minutes for the flavour to develop. Add the cumin and oregano and cook, stirring, for a minute or two, until the cumin is fragrant.

Deglaze the pan with the wine, then add the capsicum mixture to the braising pot. Leave to simmer for 30 minutes.

Remove the beef from the saucepan and pull it into shreds, using two forks. Mix the beef back into the braise, along with the olives. Simmer for a final 5 minutes.

Allow to stand for 10 minutes, before serving with cooked rice and warm tortillas.

1 kg (2 lb 3 oz) beef skirt steak
olive oil, for pan-frying
1 large red onion, sliced
2 small carrots, roughly chopped
2 celery stalks, roughly chopped
3 garlic cloves, lightly crushed
1 bay leaf
400 g (14 oz) tinned crushed
    tomatoes
1 tablespoon cider vinegar
500 ml (17 fl oz/2 cups) beef stock
2 green capsicums (bell peppers),
    sliced into 1 cm (½ inch) strips
1 red capsicum (bell pepper), sliced
    into 1 cm (½ inch) strips
2 tablespoons tomato paste
    (concentrated purée)
1 teaspoon ground cumin
½ teaspoon dried oregano
125 ml (4 fl oz/½ cup) dry white
    wine
85 g (3 oz/½ cup) pitted green olives,
    halved

TO SERVE
cooked white rice
warm tortillas

Beef & Pork Meatloaf with Buttermilk Mash

SERVES 6–8

Fill a baking dish with water and place on the lowest shelf of the oven. Preheat the oven to 160°C/320°F (fan-forced).

Whisk the eggs, buttermilk, vinegar, honey, salt, pepper and smoked and sweet paprika together in a large bowl. Add the beef, pork, garlic, onion, carrot, parsley and breadcrumbs and mix well.

Brush a rectangular baking dish with olive oil. Form the meat mixture into a loaf shape in the dish, then brush the loaf with 2 teaspoons olive oil. Place in the oven and bake for 20 minutes.

Reduce the oven temperature to 140°C/275°F (fan-forced). Bake the meatloaf for a further 90 minutes, topping up the water in the baking dish as needed.

Meanwhile, make the buttermilk mash. Place the potatoes and sweet potatoes in a saucepan and just cover with cold water. Add the salt and bring to the boil, then reduce the heat to low and simmer for about 30 minutes, or until tender. Drain the water and add the butter. Mash the potatoes. Warm the buttermilk in a small saucepan, then add to the potatoes, season with freshly ground black pepper and stir in until well blended. Keep warm.

To make the smoky glaze, heat a frying pan over high heat and add the tomatoes, onion and garlic. Cook, turning frequently, until the vegetables and garlic are charred. Cool slightly, peel the garlic, then place in a blender with the tomatoes, onion and chilli. Blend until smooth.

Wipe out the pan and return the blended tomato mixture to the pan with the sugar and salt. Cook over medium heat for 4–5 minutes, or until slightly thickened, stirring occasionally.

Arrange the mashed potatoes and steamed green beans on a serving platter. Slice the meatloaf thickly and add to the platter. Pour the smoky glaze over the meatloaf and serve.

2 free-range eggs
1 tablespoon buttermilk
1 tablespoon cider vinegar
1 teaspoon honey
1½ teaspoons sea salt flakes
½ teaspoon freshly ground black pepper
2 teaspoons smoked paprika
2 teaspoons sweet paprika
500 g (1 lb 2 oz) minced (ground) beef
500 g (1 lb 2 oz) minced (ground) pork
3 garlic cloves, crushed
1 red onion, finely diced
1 carrot, grated
15 g (½ oz/½ cup) finely chopped flat-leaf (Italian) parsley
45 g (1½ oz/¾ cup) panko breadcrumbs
olive oil, for brushing
steamed green beans, to serve

BUTTERMILK MASH
1 kg (2 lb 3 oz) mashing potatoes, peeled and cut into large chunks
500 g (1 lb 2 oz) sweet potatoes, peeled and cut into large chunks
1 teaspoon sea salt flakes
1 tablespoon butter
250 ml (8½ fl oz/1 cup) buttermilk

SMOKY GLAZE
250 g (9 oz) cherry tomatoes
1 small onion, quartered
3 garlic cloves, unpeeled
1 tinned chipotle chilli in adobo sauce
3 tablespoons soft brown sugar
¼ teaspoon sea salt flakes

Sticky Five-Spice Beef Ribs

SERVES 4

Combine the marinade ingredients in a shallow bowl.

Put the five-spice powder ingredients in a small food processor or spice grinder. Blend to a fine powder, then add to the marinade, mixing well.

Add the ribs to the marinade, coating well on all sides. Cover and leave to marinate for 1 hour.

Preheat the oven to 120°C/250°F (fan-forced).

In a heavy-based saucepan, flameproof casserole or cast-iron dish, brown the ribs over high heat, in batches if necessary. Reduce the heat, then return all the ribs to the pan, along with the marinade and 500 ml (17 fl oz/2 cups) water.

Put the lid on, then transfer to the oven and cook for 3¼ hours, or until the ribs are very tender and the meat is falling from the bone.

Meanwhile, pickle the cucumber. Combine the vinegar, sugar and salt in a small saucepan. Pour in 125 ml (4 fl oz/½ cup) water and stir over medium heat to dissolve the sugar. Bring to a simmer. Place the cucumbers in a heatproof ceramic or glass bowl and pour the liquid over. Gently press on the cucumbers to keep them submerged. Allow to cool for 1 hour, then cover and chill completely in the fridge. Drain just before using.

When the ribs are done, remove them from the sauce, to a platter; cover and leave to rest. Stir the brown sugar and vinegar into the sauce and simmer for 15 minutes, or until syrupy.

Spoon the sticky sauce over the ribs. Garnish with coriander and serve with the pickled cucumber and steamed rice.

The pickled cucumber will keep in an airtight container in the fridge for up to a week.

1.5 kg (3 lb 5 oz) beef short ribs
110 g (4 oz/½ cup, firmly packed) soft brown sugar
1 tablespoon chinkiang black vinegar, malt vinegar or rice vinegar
coriander (cilantro) leaves, to garnish
steamed white rice, to serve

MARINADE
125 ml (4 fl oz/½ cup) dark soy sauce
125 ml (4 fl oz/½ cup) light soy sauce
165 g (6 oz/¾ cup, firmly packed) soft brown sugar
4 garlic cloves, crushed
4 cm (1½ inch) piece of fresh ginger, peeled, then finely grated or chopped
½ teaspoon sea salt flakes
1 red chilli, finely chopped

FIVE-SPICE POWDER
1 cinnamon stick
1 star anise
½ teaspoon fennel seeds
½ teaspoon whole cloves
½ teaspoon sichuan peppercorns

PICKLED CUCUMBER
125 ml (4 fl oz/½ cup) rice vinegar
55 g (2 oz/¼ cup) sugar
1½ teaspoons salt
2 Lebanese (short) cucumbers, sliced lengthways, seeds removed, then thinly sliced

Osso Bucco with Gremolata

SERVES 4

Preheat the oven to 140°C/275°F (fan-forced). Heat the butter in a large heavy-based flameproof casserole dish with a tight-fitting lid. Cook the celery, carrot and onion over medium heat, stirring occasionally, for 8–10 minutes, or until softened. Add the tomato paste and cook for a further 2 minutes. Add the garlic and lemon rind strips, stir until fragrant, then remove from the heat.

In a large frying pan, heat the olive oil over medium–high heat. Toss the veal in the flour, shaking off the excess. Fry the veal, in batches if necessary, for 6–8 minutes, or until well browned on both sides. Place the veal in the casserole dish, in a single layer on top of the vegetables.

Drain most of the fat from the frying pan. Add the wine to the frying pan and simmer for 2 minutes, scraping up any bits stuck to the base of the pan. Pour the mixture over the veal, along with the tomatoes and stock; the veal should be just covered in liquid, so add a little more stock or water if necessary. Add the bay leaves and thyme. Return the casserole to the heat and bring to the boil.

Put the lid on, transfer to the oven and cook for 1½–2 hours, or until the veal is tender. It should be falling from the bone, but still holding its shape. If the cooking liquid is a little thin at this point, carefully transfer the veal to a plate and cover with foil to keep warm. Return the casserole to the stovetop and boil the sauce until thickened to the desired consistency. Return the veal to the casserole to coat in the sauce.

Meanwhile, for the gremolata, finely chop the anchovy and garlic together. Combine in a small bowl with the parsley and lemon zest.

Serve the osso bucco and sauce scattered with the gremolata, with your choice of accompaniment.

Use beef osso bucco if veal is unavailable. It is likely to be larger in size, so may also take a little longer to cook.

50 g (1¾ oz) butter
2 celery stalks, finely diced
2 carrots, finely diced
2 onions, finely diced
2 tablespoons tomato paste (concentrated purée)
2 garlic cloves, crushed
2 finely pared lemon rind strips
2 tablespoons olive oil
35 g (1¼ oz/¼ cup) plain (all-purpose) flour
8 veal osso bucco, about 1.5 kg (3 lb 5 oz) in total
250 ml (8½ fl oz/1 cup) dry white wine
400 g (14 oz) tinned crushed tomatoes
250 ml (8½ fl oz/1 cup) beef stock or water
2 bay leaves
1 thyme sprig
soft polenta or mashed potato, to serve

GREMOLATA
1 anchovy fillet
1 small garlic clove, peeled
3 tablespoons coarsely chopped flat-leaf (Italian) parsley
2 teaspoons grated lemon zest

Barbecued Beef Brisket

Combine the dry rub ingredients in a small bowl, mixing well. Rub the mixture all over the beef. At this point you can wrap the beef in plastic wrap and cure it overnight in the refrigerator, or continue with the recipe.

To make the barbecue sauce, heat the olive oil in a frying pan and cook the onion, celery and garlic for 5 minutes, until softened, stirring often. Add the stock and simmer for about 10 minutes, or until reduced by half. Leave to cool slightly, then transfer the mixture to a blender. Add the remaining barbecue sauce ingredients and blend until smooth.

Mix half the barbecue sauce with 500 ml (17 fl oz/2 cups) water. Place the beef in a shallow roasting tin and pour the sauce mixture around the sides. Cover tightly with baking paper, then a sheet of foil.

Set up a charcoal grill for indirect grilling and preheat it to low. You will need to cover the grill while cooking. Put the roasting tin in place, pull the lid down and cook the beef for 5–6 hours, or until the meat is very tender.

Increase the heat in the barbecue grill to medium–high.

Remove the brisket from the roasting tin and place on the grill to char. Cover with the lid and cook for about 20 minutes, turning the meat carefully, until lightly charred all over. Remove the beef from the heat, then cover and leave to rest for 15 minutes.

Meanwhile, pour the roasting juices into a small saucepan, stir in the remaining barbecue sauce and cook over medium–low heat until syrupy.

Slice the rested beef across the grain. Transfer to a serving platter and pour the barbecue sauce over. Serve as part of a buffet meal, or with coleslaw and fresh white buns.

Instead of cooking the brisket using a charcoal grill, you can bake it in a preheated 140°C/275°F (fan-forced) oven for the same length of time, then char it in a large grill pan or frying pan.

SERVES 12

3 kg (6 lb 10 oz) beef brisket,
  with fat cap intact
coleslaw, to serve
fresh white bread buns, to serve

DRY RUB
1 tablespoon chilli powder
1 teaspoon ground cumin
1 teaspoon mustard powder
2 teaspoons soft brown sugar
1 tablespoon sea salt flakes
1 teaspoon freshly ground black
  pepper

BARBECUE SAUCE
1 tablespoon olive oil
1 small red onion, finely chopped
1 stalk celery, chopped
2 garlic cloves, crushed
250 ml (8½ fl oz/1 cup) beef stock
200 ml (7 fl oz) tomato ketchup
50 ml (1¾ fl oz) worcestershire sauce
1 tablespoon cider vinegar
2 teaspoons hot English mustard
2 teaspoons smoked paprika

Beef, Stout & Black Pepper Stew

SERVES 6–8

Toss the beef in the flour, shaking off the excess. Heat the olive oil in a large heavy-based saucepan over medium–high heat. Brown the beef in batches, then return all the meat and any juices to the pan.

Add the carrot, onion and garlic to the pan. Stir in the tomato paste, stout, stock, pepper and salt. Stir well and bring to the boil. Put the lid on, then reduce the heat to low and simmer for 1¼ hours, or until the beef is almost tender.

Remove the lid and cook, uncovered, for a further 30 minutes, or until the beef is very tender but still holding its shape, and the sauce is slightly thickened.

Serve with mashed potato and steamed greens.

This stew can also be cooked in the oven. Prepare the stew in a large flameproof casserole dish that has a tight-fitting lid. When the stock and stout have been added to the stew, and it has come to the boil on the stovetop, put the lid on and cook in a preheated 140°C/275°F (fan-forced) oven for 1½–2 hours, or until the beef is tender.

Leftovers freeze really well. Store in freezer-safe containers and use within 6–8 weeks.

1.5 kg (3 lb 5 oz) oyster blade steak, diced
35 g (1¼ oz/¼ cup) plain (all-purpose) flour
60 ml (2 fl oz/¼ cup) olive oil
2 carrots, roughly chopped
2 onions, sliced
3 garlic cloves, sliced
2 tablespoons tomato paste (concentrated purée)
375 ml (12½ fl oz/1½ cups) stout
250 ml (8½ fl oz/1 cup) beef stock
2 teaspoons freshly ground black pepper
pinch of sea salt flakes
mashed potato, to serve
steamed greens, to serve

Chipotle & Chorizo Chilli Con Carne

SERVES 4

Heat the olive oil in a large heavy-based saucepan over medium heat. Add the onion and garlic and cook for 3 minutes, or until softened. Crumble the chorizo into the pan, add the cumin and paprika and cook, stirring, for 2–3 minutes, or until the chorizo is cooked.

Stir in the chipotle chilli, bay leaf, tomatoes and stock and bring to a simmer. Stir in the beef, then cover the pan and cook over low heat for 30 minutes.

Add the beans, lime juice, chocolate, coriander and 500 ml (17 fl oz/ 2 cups) water. Cover and continue to cook for a further 1½ hours, stirring occasionally, and adding more water if necessary. The consistency should be thick but not too dry. Season to taste with sea salt flakes and freshly ground black pepper.

Serve with cooked white rice, topped with tomato, avocado and coriander leaves.

2 tablespoons olive oil
1 red onion, finely chopped
2 garlic cloves, crushed
1 fresh Mexican chorizo sausage, skin removed
1 teaspoon ground cumin
1 teaspoon smoked paprika
1 tinned chipotle chilli in adobo sauce, chopped
1 bay leaf
400 g (14 oz) tinned crushed tomatoes
125 ml (4 fl oz/½ cup) beef stock
500 g (1 lb 2 oz) stewing steak, cut into large cubes
110 g (4 oz/½ cup) dried black beans, rinsed
juice of 1 lime
2 squares dark chocolate
1 handful coriander (cilantro) leaves and stems, chopped

TO SERVE
cooked white rice
1 tomato, chopped
1 avocado, chopped
coriander (cilantro) leaves, to garnish

Beef Cheeks Braised in Red Wine

SERVES 4

Season the beef cheeks on both sides with sea salt flakes and freshly ground black pepper.

Heat a large heavy-based saucepan or flameproof casserole dish until hot. Add 1 tablespoon of the olive oil and brown the beef cheeks over high heat for a good 3–4 minutes on each side. Remove to a plate.

Add the remaining oil to the pan. Reduce the heat to low and cook the onion, garlic, carrot and celery for 5–7 minutes, until softened.

Return the beef to the pan. Add the bay leaves and thyme sprigs. Pour in the wine and stock, then put the lid on. Bring to a simmer and cook over low heat for 3 hours, or until the beef cheeks are starting to fall apart.

Remove the lid. Simmer, uncovered, for a further 20–25 minutes, or until the sauce has reduced and thickened slightly. During this time, taste the sauce and add the vincotto or balsamic vinegar for a more intense, sweet flavour, if desired.

Remove the bay leaves and thyme sprigs, stripping off the thyme leaves and stirring them back into the stew.

Scatter the parsley over and serve with your choice of accompaniment.

4 beef cheeks, about 1 kg (2 lb 3 oz) in total
60 ml (2 fl oz/¼ cup) olive oil
1 large brown onion, finely chopped
4 garlic cloves, finely chopped
2 carrots, chopped
2 celery stalks, chopped
3 bay leaves
3 large thyme sprigs
500 ml (17 fl oz/2 cups) shiraz or full-bodied red wine
500 ml (17 fl oz/2 cups) beef stock
1–2 tablespoons vincotto, or sticky good-quality balsamic vinegar (optional)
chopped flat-leaf (Italian) parsley, to serve
creamy mashed potato, soft polenta or cooked pasta, to serve

LAMB

Middle Eastern Leg of Lamb with Couscous Salad

SERVES 4–6

Preheat the oven to 140°C/275°F (fan-forced).

Arrange the onion slices in a roasting dish and place the lamb leg on top.

In a small bowl, mix the marinade ingredients together until well combined, then pour over the lamb. Pour 125 ml (4 fl oz/½ cup) water into the base of the roasting dish. Cover tightly with baking paper, then a sheet of foil. Transfer to the oven and cook for 3 hours.

Remove the foil and paper. Baste the lamb with the pan juices, then roast for a further 30 minutes to brown. Remove from the oven and rest for 15 minutes before carving.

To make the salad, put the couscous in a mixing bowl with the salt and cumin. Pour 250 ml (8½ fl oz/1 cup) boiling water over and cover the bowl tightly with plastic wrap. Rest for 5 minutes, then fluff the couscous grains with a fork and allow to cool. Add the chickpeas, spring onion, parsley, mint, cucumber, pomegranate seeds, almonds and feta. Drizzle with the olive oil and lemon juice, and toss to combine well. Leave at room temperature until the lamb has rested.

Carve the lamb and arrange on a platter. Pour a spoonful of pan juices over the meat and serve with the couscous salad.

2 onions, sliced into thick rings
1 lamb leg, bone in, weighing about
  2 kg (4 lb 6 oz)

MARINADE
zest and juice of 1 lemon
60 ml (2 fl oz/¼ cup) pomegranate
  syrup
3 garlic cloves, crushed
1 teaspoon ground cumin
1 teaspoon sea salt flakes
½ teaspoon ground cinnamon
½ teaspoon sweet paprika

COUSCOUS SALAD
185 g (6½ oz/1 cup) couscous
½ teaspoon sea salt flakes
½ teaspoon ground cumin
400 g (14 oz) tinned chickpeas, rinsed
  and drained
3 spring onions (scallions), thinly
  sliced
15 g (½ oz/½ cup) finely chopped
  flat-leaf (Italian) parsley
25 g (1 oz/½ cup) chopped mint
  leaves
1 Lebanese (short) cucumber, finely
  diced
seeds from ½ pomegranate
80 g (2¾ oz/½ cup) raw almonds,
  chopped
50 g (1¾ oz/⅓ cup) crumbled feta
1 tablespoon olive oil
juice of 1 lemon

Lamb Vindaloo Curry with Cucumber Salad

SERVES 4

Start by making the marinade. Heat a small dry frying pan over medium heat. Add the cumin, mustard, fenugreek and coriander seeds and toast for a minute, or until fragrant. Grind the seeds using a mortar and pestle, then tip into a mixing bowl. Add the garlic, ginger, vinegar and peanut oil and stir to blend well.

Add the lamb to the marinade, stirring until well coated. Cover and marinate in the fridge for 2 hours.

Heat the peanut oil in a saucepan over medium heat. Add the onion and cook, stirring, for about 5 minutes, or until softened and turning golden brown.

Add the marinated lamb, along with the chillies. Cook, turning occasionally, to brown the lamb on all sides. Add the cinnamon stick, bay leaf, cardamom pod, turmeric, sugar, salt and pepper. Pour in 500 ml (17 fl oz/2 cups) water, stirring to mix the spices through.

Bring to the boil, reduce the heat, then cover and simmer for 1½ hours, or until the lamb is tender.

Meanwhile, prepare the salad. Leaving the skin on, cut the cucumbers in half lengthways and remove the seeds. Slice thinly into half-rounds and place in a mixing bowl. Sprinkle with the salt and toss well, then transfer to a colander and leave to drain for 20 minutes.

Combine the yoghurt, lemon, garlic and mint in a bowl, add the drained cucumber and mix well.

Serve the curry over steamed rice, with the cucumber salad on the side.

1 kg (2 lb 3 oz) boneless lamb shoulder, cut into 3 cm (1¼ inch) cubes
1 tablespoon peanut oil
1 onion, finely chopped
3 small dried red chillies
1 cinnamon stick
1 bay leaf
1 cardamom pod
½ teaspoon ground turmeric
1 teaspoon soft brown sugar
1 teaspoon sea salt flakes
½ teaspoon freshly ground black pepper
steamed white rice, to serve

MARINADE
1 teaspoon cumin seeds
1 teaspoon black mustard seeds
1 teaspoon fenugreek seeds
2 teaspoons coriander seeds
3 garlic cloves, crushed
3 cm (1¼ inch) piece of fresh ginger, peeled and grated
1 tablespoon apple cider vinegar
1 tablespoon peanut oil

CUCUMBER SALAD
5 Lebanese (short) cucumbers
1 teaspoon sea salt
250 g (9 oz/1 cup) plain yoghurt
2 teaspoons lemon juice
1 garlic clove, crushed
1 tablespoon finely chopped mint leaves

Red Wine & Rosemary Lamb Shanks with Cauliflower Purée

SERVES 4

Preheat the oven to 130°C/265°F (fan-forced).

Place the flour in a shallow dish, mixing the salt and pepper through. Add the lamb shanks and toss to coat, shaking off any excess flour.

Heat a large flameproof casserole dish over high heat. Add the olive oil and brown the lamb shanks all over, then remove to a plate.

Reduce the heat to medium and cook the onion, carrot and celery for 2 minutes, stirring and adding a little more oil if required. Add the garlic and rosemary and cook for a further minute.

Add the sugar, wine, vinegar, passata, orange zest, orange juice and 250 ml (8½ fl oz/1 cup) water. Stir well, scraping up any bits sticking to the bottom of the dish. Return the shanks and any juices to the dish.

Cover with baking paper and put the lid on. Transfer to the oven and bake for 2 hours. Stir the mixture, turn the shanks over, then cover and bake for a further 2 hours, or until the meat is very tender.

To make the cauliflower purée, bring a saucepan of water to the boil over high heat. Add the cauliflower and cook for 10 minutes, or until tender. Drain, then add the sour cream, salt and pepper. Allow to cool slightly, then transfer to a blender and purée until smooth.

Serve the lamb shanks and sauce with the cauliflower purée and steamed green beans.

35 g (1¼ oz/¼ cup) plain (all-purpose) flour
1 teaspoon sea salt flakes
1 teaspoon freshly ground black pepper
4 French-trimmed lamb shanks
2 tablespoons olive oil, approximately
1 onion, finely diced
1 carrot, finely diced
2 celery stalks, finely diced
2 garlic cloves, crushed
4 rosemary sprigs
1 teaspoon soft brown sugar
250 ml (8½ fl oz/1 cup) shiraz or dry red wine
2 tablespoons balsamic vinegar
250 ml (8½ fl oz/1 cup) tomato passata
zest and juice of 1 orange
steamed green beans, to serve

CAULIFLOWER PURÉE
½ cauliflower, broken into florets
2 tablespoons sour cream
½ teaspoon sea salt flakes
pinch of freshly ground black pepper

Moroccan Lamb Stew

Combine the marinade ingredients in a mixing bowl and stir to blend well. Add the lamb and mix well to coat it in the spices. Cover and allow to marinate at room temperature for 30 minutes.

Preheat the oven to 130°C/265°F (fan-forced).

Heat the olive oil in a flameproof casserole dish over medium heat. Working in two batches, brown the lamb all over, then remove to a plate.

Reduce the heat to medium and cook the onion and capsicum for 5 minutes, stirring occasionally. Return the lamb and any juices to the dish. Add the tomatoes, sweet potato, honey, apricots, salt and bay leaves. Pour in 375 ml (12½ fl oz/1½ cups) water, stirring to mix the spices through. Put the lid on, transfer to the oven and bake for 1½ hours.

Stir the chickpeas into the stew, adding a little water if it looks a bit dry. Replace the lid and bake for a further 1½ hours, or until the lamb is very tender.

Serve the stew in deep bowls, with a dollop of yoghurt and garnish with coriander leaves.

SERVES 4–6

600 g (1 lb 5 oz) boneless lamb shoulder, cut into 5 cm (2 inch) chunks
1 tablespoon olive oil
2 onions, chopped
1 red capsicum (bell pepper), sliced
3 large tomatoes, roughly chopped
1 sweet potato, peeled and cut into large chunks
1 tablespoon honey
45 g (1½ oz/¼ cup) dried apricots
1½ teaspoons sea salt flakes
2 bay leaves
400 g (14 oz) tinned chickpeas, rinsed and drained
185 g (6½ oz/¾ cup) plain yoghurt
coriander (cilantro) leaves, to garnish

MARINADE
1 tablespoon sweet paprika
1 tablespoon ground turmeric
1 teaspoon ground cinnamon
1 teaspoon ground cumin
½ teaspoon freshly ground black pepper
2 garlic cloves, crushed
3 cm (1¼ inch) piece of fresh ginger, peeled and grated
1 tablespoon olive oil
1 tablespoon cider vinegar

Asian-Style Sticky Lamb Ribs

SERVES 4

Preheat the oven to 130°C/265°F (fan-forced).

Find a baking dish large enough to hold both racks of lamb; each lamb rack can be cut in half, if required, to fit your baking dish.

In a small bowl, combine the garlic, ginger, chilli, kecap manis, oyster sauce, soy sauce, palm sugar, sesame oil and lime juice. Brush the mixture over the lamb, then transfer the lamb to the baking dish.

Discard the dry leafy tops from the lemongrass stalks. Bruise the white stem of each one with the back of a knife, then cut each lemongrass stem into three pieces. Add to the baking dish with the star anise.

Cover the dish tightly with baking paper and a sheet of foil. Transfer to the oven and bake for 2 hours. Carefully remove the paper and foil, then turn the ribs over. Seal up tightly again, then bake for a further 1 hour.

Remove the lamb from the oven. Leave to cool slightly, then use a sharp knife to cut the lamb into segments between the ribs.

Serve on a platter, sprinkled with the spring onion and toasted sesame seeds, with steamed rice and bok choy alongside.

Kecap manis is a dark, thick, sweet Indonesian soy sauce, available from Asian grocery stores.

2 x 800 g (1 lb 12 oz) racks of lamb ribs
3 garlic cloves, crushed
2 tablespoons peeled and grated fresh ginger
1 long red chilli, finely chopped
60 ml (2 fl oz/¼ cup) kecap manis (see tip)
2 tablespoons oyster sauce
2 tablespoons dark soy sauce
2 tablespoons palm sugar (jaggery)
1 teaspoon sesame oil
juice of 2 limes
2 lemongrass stalks
2 star anise
4 spring onions (scallions), sliced finely
1 tablespoon sesame seeds, toasted
steamed jasmine rice, to serve
steamed bok choy, to serve

West Indian Lamb Curry with Coconut Rice

SERVES 4–6

Combine the curry powder, salt, pepper, garlic, ginger and lime juice in a mixing bowl. Add the lamb and toss to coat well in the spices. Cover and marinate in the fridge for 2 hours.

Heat the peanut oil in a large heavy-based saucepan over high heat. Add the lamb and stir to coat it in the oil. Put the lid on, reduce the heat to low and cook for 30 minutes.

Add the onion and cook, stirring, for 6–8 minutes, or until softened. Stir in 250 ml (8½ fl oz/1 cup) of the stock, add the allspice berries, then cover and cook for a further 1 hour.

Stir in the chillies, capsicums, spring onion, coriander and remaining stock. Cover and continue to simmer over low heat for a further 1 hour.

Add the sweet potato and potato, and a little water if the curry is dry. Cover and simmer for a further 30 minutes.

To make the coconut rice, place the rice, coconut milk and 500 ml (17 fl oz/2 cups) water in a saucepan. Bring to the boil over medium heat, reduce the heat to low, then cover and simmer for 10 minutes. Stand, covered, for 10 minutes before serving.

Serve the curry and coconut rice in deep dishes, garnished with the extra coriander leaves.

2 tablespoons mild curry powder
2 teaspoons sea salt flakes
½ teaspoon freshly ground black pepper
2 garlic cloves, crushed
4 cm (1½ inch) piece of fresh ginger, peeled and grated
juice of 1 lime
800 g (1 lb 12 oz) boneless lamb shoulder, cut into large chunks
60 ml (2 fl oz/¼ cup) peanut oil
1 onion, roughly chopped
500 ml (17 fl oz/2 cups) vegetable stock
6 allspice berries
1–2 small hot red chillies
1 small green capsicum (bell pepper), sliced
1 small red capsicum (bell pepper), sliced
2 spring onions (scallions), sliced
3 tablespoons chopped coriander (cilantro) leaves and stems, plus extra leaves to garnish
1 sweet potato, peeled and cut into 4 chunks
1 potato, peeled and quartered

COCONUT RICE
400 g (14 oz/2 cups) long-grain white rice
250 ml (8½ fl oz/1 cup) coconut milk

Slow-Roasted Greek Lamb Shoulder

SERVES 6

Preheat the oven to 140°C/275°F (fan-forced). Drizzle 2 tablespoons of the olive oil into a deep roasting dish. Add the potato and onion slices, tossing to coat them with the oil and spreading them around the pan. Sprinkle with sea salt flakes and freshly ground black pepper.

Arrange three garlic cloves, three rosemary sprigs, one of the bay leaves and half the lemon slices over the potatoes to form a bed for the lamb. Sprinkle with half the oregano.

Heat the remaining oil in a large non-stick frying pan over high heat. Sprinkle the lamb well with sea salt and cook for 4–5 minutes on each side, or until well browned. Place in the roasting dish and scatter with the remaining garlic, herbs and lemon slices.

Pour most of the fat from the frying pan. Add the stock to the pan and cook over medium heat, scraping up all the tasty bits from the bottom of the pan. Carefully pour the mixture into the roasting dish.

Dot the butter evenly over the lamb and potatoes. Cover the dish with baking paper, then seal with foil. Transfer to the oven and roast for 3½–4 hours, or until the lamb is very tender.

Remove the roasting dish from the oven. Increase the oven temperature to 180°C/350°F (fan-forced).

Remove the foil and baking paper from the dish. Carefully pour off the juices for a delicious sauce, skimming off the fat when it has had a chance to settle. Return the roasting dish to the oven and roast the lamb for a further 10–15 minutes, or until well browned.

Transfer the lamb to a plate, cover loosely with foil and leave to rest for 20 minutes before serving.

Meanwhile, return the potatoes to the oven again to allow the top layer to become crispy. Serve the lamb with the potatoes, pan juices and extra lemon wedges.

60 ml (2 fl oz/¼ cup) olive oil
6 boiling potatoes, such as desiree, Dutch cream, kipfler (fingerling) or pink eye, scrubbed and thinly sliced
1 onion, thinly sliced
6 garlic cloves, skin on, smashed
6 rosemary sprigs
2 bay leaves
1 lemon, sliced, plus extra wedges to serve
1 tablespoon dried Greek oregano
1 lamb shoulder, about 2 kg (4 lb 6 oz), jointed by your butcher
500 ml (17 fl oz/2 cups) lamb stock, chicken stock or water
40 g (1½ oz) butter, softened

Cinnamon Lamb Casserole with Risoni

SERVES 4

Preheat the oven to 140°C/275°F (fan-forced).

Heat the olive oil in a large heavy-based saucepan over high heat.

Working in batches, brown the lamb evenly all over, then transfer to a low-sided casserole dish or baking dish.

Reduce the heat under the saucepan to low and cook the onion, stirring, for 4–5 minutes, or until softened. Add the eggplant, garlic, cinnamon sticks, lemon peel, herbs, salt and pepper. Cook, stirring, for a further 2–3 minutes, then deglaze the pan with 250 ml (8½ fl oz/1 cup) of the stock, releasing any bits stuck to the bottom. Pour the mixture over the lamb.

Stir in the tomatoes and remaining stock. Cover the dish tightly with baking paper and a sheet of foil, then transfer to the oven and bake for 2 hours.

Remove the paper and foil. Stir in the lemon juice and risoni, adding a little water if necessary. Bake for a further 30 minutes, or until the pasta is cooked.

Remove from the oven and allow to stand for 10 minutes before serving. Serve with a fresh green salad.

2 tablespoons olive oil
600 g (1 lb 5 oz) boneless lamb shoulder, cut into 3 cm (1¼ inch) chunks
1 onion, diced
1 eggplant (aubergine), roughly chopped
3 garlic cloves, crushed
2 cinnamon sticks
1 thick lemon peel strip
4 oregano sprigs
3 thyme sprigs
2 bay leaves
1½ teaspoons sea salt flakes
½ teaspoon freshly ground black pepper
500 ml (17 fl oz/2 cups) chicken stock
400 g (14 oz) tinned crushed tomatoes
juice of 1 lemon
100 g (3½ oz/½ cup) risoni
fresh green salad, to serve

Moussaka

Preheat the oven to 200°C/400°F (fan-forced). Place the whole capsicums on an oven rack and roast for 20 minutes, or until the skins are blackened. Remove the capsicums to a small bowl, cover and allow to cool. When cool enough to handle, discard the capsicum stalks, skin, ribs and seeds. Finely chop the flesh and set aside.

Heat 2 tablespoons olive oil in a large saucepan over medium heat. Add the onion, garlic, bay leaves and cinnamon sticks and cook, stirring occasionally, for about 6 minutes. Add the lamb and cook until browned, stirring to break up the lumps. Add the veal and continue to cook, stirring, until browned. Stir in the salt, oregano, cumin and roasted capsicum and cook for 5 minutes, stirring occasionally.

Stir in the tomatoes and vinegar. Put the lid on, reduce the heat to a simmer and cook for 40 minutes, adding a little water if needed. While the sauce is simmering, heat a large grill pan or frying pan over high heat. Brush the eggplant slices with olive oil and cook for a few minutes on each side, or until well browned. Dust the warm eggplant slices with a light sprinkling of cinnamon and set aside.

To make the béchamel sauce, melt the butter in a saucepan over low heat. Stir in the flour and cook, stirring, for 1–2 minutes. Add the milk, one-third at a time, stirring between additions until smooth. Stir in the salt, nutmeg and cloves, then simmer over low heat, stirring occasionally, for 10 minutes. Remove from the heat and stir in the cheese.

Preheat the oven to 160°C/320°F (fan-forced). To assemble the moussaka, place one-third of the eggplant slices in the base of a lightly greased baking dish. Spread half the tomato sauce mixture over the top. Add half the remaining eggplant slices, then top with the remaining tomato sauce mixture. Layer the remaining eggplant slices over the top, then cover with the béchamel sauce.

Bake for 1 hour, or until golden brown on top. Remove from the oven and allow to stand for 15 minutes before serving, for the moussaka to set.

SERVES 8–10

2 red capsicums (bell peppers)
2 tablespoons olive oil, plus extra
  for brushing
2 onions, finely chopped
2 garlic cloves, crushed
2 bay leaves
2 cinnamon sticks
500 g (1 lb 2 oz) minced (ground)
  lamb
500 g (1 lb 2 oz) minced (ground)
  veal
2 teaspoons sea salt flakes
2 teaspoons dried oregano
1 teaspoon ground cumin
800 g (1 lb 12 oz) tinned crushed
  tomatoes
1 tablespoon cider vinegar
4 small eggplants (aubergines),
  cut into ½ cm (¼ inch) slices
ground cinnamon, for dusting

BÉCHAMEL SAUCE
100 g (3½ oz) butter
75 g (2¼ oz/½ cup) plain
  (all-purpose) flour
750 ml (25½ fl oz/3 cups) whole milk
½ teaspoon sea salt flakes
⅛ teaspoon ground nutmeg
⅛ teaspoon ground cloves
100 g (3½ oz) grated kefalograviera,
  or another hard salty sheep's cheese
  such as Pecorino Romano, parmesan
  or kefalotyri

DESSERT

Roasted Peach Cake

SERVES 8–10

Preheat the oven to 180°C/350°F (fan-forced). Line a baking tray with baking paper.

Place the peaches on the baking tray, brush lightly with the melted butter and roast in the oven for 8–10 minutes. Allow to cool.

Reduce the oven temperature to 140°C/275°F (fan-forced). Grease a 25 cm (10 inch) springform cake tin and line the base and side with baking paper.

Using a stand mixer fitted with the paddle attachment, beat the butter, brown sugar and caster sugar for 2 minutes. Scrape down the side of the bowl and continue mixing for a further 2 minutes, or until the mixture becomes lighter in colour. Add an egg and beat in well. Scrape down the side of the bowl, then add the second egg and beat for 30 seconds. Add the orange zest, yoghurt and vinegar and beat on low speed until combined.

Sift the flour, baking powder and salt together, then add to the batter in two batches, folding in with a spatula between additions.

Pour half the batter into the cake tin. Arrange half the peach pieces on top, then cover with the remaining batter. Top with the remaining peach quarters and sprinkle with an extra 1 tablespoon brown sugar. Cover the tin with baking paper and secure with ovenproof twine.

Bake for 1 hour, then carefully remove the twine and paper. Bake for a further 20 minutes, or until a skewer inserted into the middle of the cake comes out clean.

Allow to cool in the tin for 15 minutes, before removing from the tin.

Serve at room temperature, with thick cream or vanilla ice cream.

This cake can be refrigerated in an airtight container, and is best enjoyed within three days.

6 large yellow peaches, cut into quarters
2 teaspoons melted butter
thick (double/heavy) cream or vanilla ice cream, to serve

CAKE
125 g (4½ oz) butter
140 g (5 oz/¾ cup, loosely packed) soft brown sugar, plus extra for sprinkling
55 g (2 oz/¼ cup) caster (superfine) sugar
2 large free-range eggs
finely grated zest of 1 orange
125 g (4½ oz/½ cup) plain yoghurt
2 teaspoons apple cider vinegar
150 g (5½ oz/1 cup) plain (all-purpose) flour
1 teaspoon baking powder
¼ teaspoon sea salt

Sticky Rice in Banana Leaves with Coconut Jam

MAKES ABOUT
20 PARCELS

Start by making the coconut jam. In a bowl, whisk the egg yolks with 2 tablespoons of the coconut cream and set aside. In a saucepan, heat the palm sugar over low heat until melted. Cook, stirring occasionally, for 4 minutes, or until the sugar is a deep golden brown. Remove from the heat and cool slightly, then stir in the remaining coconut cream. Add the pandan leaves, folding them into knots to fit in the pan.

Place the pan back over low heat, stirring until smooth. Cook for 6–7 minutes, stirring, until thickened slightly. Remove the pan from the heat. Whisk the palm sugar mixture, a tablespoon at a time, into the egg yolk mixture. Pour the mixture back into the pan and cook over low heat for about 5 minutes, or until thickened. Pour through a sieve into a bowl, then cover and chill in the fridge overnight to set.

To make the sticky rice, put the rice, coconut milk, salt, palm sugar and 250 ml (8½ fl oz/1 cup) water in a saucepan, stirring well. Heat over medium heat until boiling, then reduce the heat to low and put the lid on. Simmer for 15 minutes, then remove from the heat. Rest, covered, for 30 minutes.

Soften the banana leaves over steam, or in the microwave for 30 seconds, until the leaves are soft. Place a banana leaf portion on a board, shiny side down. Spoon a tablespoon of sticky rice onto the leaf. Add a slice of banana, and a teaspoonful of coconut jam. Cover with another tablespoonful of rice, enclosing the banana and jam filling in the rice. Fold the sides of the leaves over, then roll the parcel into a cylinder. Place in a steamer basket, seam side down. Repeat with the remaining ingredients until finished, layering them in the steamer basket.

Place the steamer basket over a saucepan of boiling water. Cover and steam the parcels for 30 minutes, adding water to the steamer as necessary. Leave until cool enough to handle before removing from the steamer. Serve hot or at room temperature.

2–3 large banana leaves, cut into 15 cm (6 inch) squares
2 ripe bananas, peeled, each cut into 10 long slices

COCONUT JAM
2 large free-range egg yolks
185 ml (6½ fl oz/¾ cup) coconut cream
75 g (2½ oz/⅓ cup) grated palm sugar (jaggery)
2 fresh pandan leaves

STICKY RICE
200 g (7 oz/1 cup) glutinous rice, rinsed and drained
250 ml (8½ fl oz/1 cup) coconut milk
pinch of sea salt flakes
50 g (1¾ oz/¼ cup) grated palm sugar (jaggery)

Chocolate Marmalade Bread & Butter Pudding

SERVES 4–6

Preheat the oven to 120°C/250°F (fan-forced). Grease a 1.75 litre (60 fl oz/7 cup) capacity shallow baking dish.

Spread one side of the bread slices with butter. Arrange in the baking dish in a couple of layers, slightly overlapping the slices, and evenly intersperse the layers with the chocolate and blobs of marmalade. Some of the marmalade can be spread on the top layer of bread.

Combine the eggs, caster sugar and vanilla in a bowl and whisk to combine. Whisk in the cream and milk until combined. Pour over the bread and leave to soak for 10 minutes, pushing the bread slices under the liquid so the crusts soften too.

Sprinkle the pudding with a little raw sugar. Place the baking dish in a large roasting dish, then pour enough very hot water into the roasting dish to reach halfway up the side of the baking dish.

Transfer to the oven and bake for 1 hour, or until the egg mixture has just set. Carefully remove from the roasting dish and leave to cool slightly.

Serve the pudding warm, drizzled with pouring cream.

The crusts on the bread give a nice texture to the pudding, but can be removed if you prefer a smoother dessert.

9 slices *pane de casa* bread, or similar bread, each about 2 cm (¾ inch) wide, cut in half to give 18 pieces
butter, for spreading
100 g (3½ oz/⅔ cup) chopped dark chocolate
160 g (5½ oz/½ cup) good-quality marmalade
5 large free-range eggs
170 g (6 oz/¾ cup) caster (superfine) sugar
1 teaspoon vanilla extract or vanilla bean paste
600 ml (20½ fl oz) thickened (whipping) cream
250 ml (8½ fl oz/1 cup) full-cream milk
raw sugar, for sprinkling
pouring (single/light) cream, to serve

Crisp Apple Crumble

SERVES 4

Preheat the oven to 160°C/320°F (fan-forced).

Melt the butter and sugar in a frying pan over low heat. Add the apples and cinnamon stick and cover the pan. Increase the heat to medium and cook for 4–5 minutes. Turn the apples over, then cover and continue to cook for 3 minutes, or until the apple becomes lightly caramelised.

Combine the crumble topping ingredients in a mixing bowl and mix with your fingertips until the mixture resembles crumbs.

Transfer the apples to a small buttered baking dish. Evenly sprinkle the crumble topping over the top.

Bake for 30 minutes, or until the topping is golden and the sauce underneath is bubbling.

Serve warm, with vanilla bean ice cream.

50 g (1¾ oz) butter, plus extra
   for greasing
2 tablespoons caster (superfine) sugar
4 eating apples, peeled, cored and cut
   into thick wedges
1 cinnamon stick
vanilla bean ice cream, to serve

CRUMBLE TOPPING
40 g (1½ oz) soft brown sugar
75 g (2¾ oz/½ cup) plain (all-
   purpose) flour
25 g (1 oz/¼ cup) ground almonds
½ teaspoon ground cinnamon
25 g (1 oz) cold butter, grated

Baked Sticky Citrus Puddings

SERVES 4

Preheat the oven to 160°C/320°F (fan-forced). Lightly grease four 350 ml (12 fl oz) capacity mugs or baking dishes.

In a clean bowl, whisk the egg whites until soft peaks form, using an electric mixer.

In a large mixing bowl, beat the egg yolks and sugar for 10 minutes, or until pale and creamy, using an electric mixer. Add the lemon and orange zest and beat well. Gently stir in the milk, then fold in the flour.

Add the butter, all the citrus juices and the beaten egg whites, and fold in carefully to avoid beating the air out of the eggs.

Pour the mixture into the prepared dishes. Place the dishes in a baking dish half-filled with hot water.

Transfer to the oven and bake for 40–45 minutes, or until the tops have set and turned golden brown. The base will be a tangy citrus curd.

Serve the puddings hot, with thick cream.

3 extra-large free-range eggs, yolks and whites separated
145 g (5 oz/⅔ cup) caster (superfine) sugar
finely grated zest of 1 lemon
finely grated zest of ½ orange
250 ml (8½ fl oz/1 cup) milk
75 g (2½ oz/½ cup) plain (all-purpose) flour, sifted
80 g (2¾ oz) butter, melted and cooled slightly
2 tablespoons lemon juice
1 tablespoon orange juice
1 tablespoon lime juice
thick (double/heavy) cream, to serve

Ricotta & Pear Cheesecake with a Macadamia Crust

SERVES 8

Preheat the oven to 160°C/320°F (fan-forced). Grease a 22 cm (8¾ inch) springform cake tin and line the base with baking paper.

To make the crust, place the cookies and macadamias in a food processor and blend to coarse crumbs. Add the butter and pulse until the mixture comes together in clumps. Press into the cake tin and bake for 10 minutes.

Remove from the oven. Reduce the oven temperature to 120°C/250°F (fan-forced).

Arrange the pears, cut side down, around the baked crust, leaving some space in between, and finish with two pear quarters in the centre.

In a large bowl, beat the ricotta and cream cheese together until smooth. Beat in the cream, vanilla, eggs and sugar until smooth.

Pour the mixture over the pears, smoothing to cover the pears and give a flat surface. Bake for 55–60 minutes, or until just set.

Leave the cake in the oven with the door slightly ajar for 2 hours, or until cooled. Chill in the fridge for 3 hours, or until cold.

Dust thickly with icing sugar and serve with thick cream, if desired.

3 just-ripe pears, peeled, cored and cut into quarters
600 g (1 lb 5 oz) fresh ricotta
250 g (9 oz) cream cheese, softened
125 ml (4 fl oz/½ cup) thickened (whipping) cream
1½ teaspoons vanilla bean paste or vanilla extract
2 large free-range eggs
170 g (6 oz/¾ cup) caster (superfine) sugar
sifted icing (confectioners') sugar, to serve
thick (double/heavy) cream, to serve (optional)

CRUST
250 g (9 oz) shortbread cookies
60 g (2 oz) macadamia nuts, toasted
70 g (2½ oz) unsalted butter, melted

Winter Warming Dried Fruit Compote

SERVES 4

Preheat the oven to 140°C/275°F (fan-forced).

Arrange the dried peaches, apricots, pears and cranberries in a casserole dish.

Put the remaining ingredients in a saucepan. Add 500 ml (17 fl oz/ 2 cups) cold water and stir over medium heat until the sugar has dissolved. Leave to simmer for 5 minutes.

Pour the sugar syrup over the fruit. Cover the casserole dish, transfer to the oven and bake for 1½ hours.

Serve the fruit compote with vanilla ice cream for dessert, or with porridge for breakfast. It will keep in an airtight container in the fridge for up to a week.

Made from the juice of unripe grapes, verjuice adds a lovely dimension to this dish. If you don't have any, you could use 60 ml (2 fl oz/¼ cup) lemon juice mixed with 185 ml (6½ fl oz/¾cup) water, or simply replace with water.

90 g (3 oz) dried peach halves
90 g (3 oz) dried apricots
90 g (3 oz) dried pears
60 g (2 oz/½ cup) dried cranberries
250 ml (8½ fl oz/1 cup) verjuice (see tip) or water
170 g (6 oz/¾ cup) caster (superfine) sugar
1 cinnamon stick
1 teaspoon vanilla bean paste

Chai Tea Spiced Slow-Baked Rice Pudding

SERVES 6

Preheat the oven to 120°C/250°F (fan-forced). Grease a 1.75 litre (60 fl oz/7 cup) capacity rectangular baking dish.

Place the rice in the base of the dish. Pour the milk over and stir in the sugar. Add the tea bags, leaving the paper tags outside the dish. Add the spices and a small pinch of sea salt flakes, stirring briefly.

Cover the dish with foil and place the dish on a baking tray. Transfer to the oven and bake for 1 hour 10 minutes.

Carefully remove the foil, then bake for a further 45–50 minutes. A skin may form on the top; if so, carefully remove the skin, without removing the spices.

Dot the chopped butter around the dish. Combine the cinnamon sugar ingredients and sprinkle half over the pudding. Return to the oven and bake for a further 15–20 minutes, or until slightly golden.

Gently remove any skin, as well as the tea bags and the spices. Stir and serve the creamy rice in bowls, with the remaining cinnamon sugar, and cream if desired.

This pudding tastes exactly like chai tea. You can serve it on its own, or with poached fruit, such as pear or quince.

110 g (4 oz/½ cup) arborio rice
1 litre (34 fl oz/4 cups) full-cream milk
55 g (2 oz/¼ cup) caster (superfine) sugar
2 black tea bags (such as English breakfast)
2 cinnamon sticks
7 cardamom pods, lightly crushed
8 black peppercorns
6 whole cloves
25 g (1 oz) butter, chopped
whipped cream or thick (double/heavy) cream, to serve (optional)

CINNAMON SUGAR
1½ tablespoons caster (superfine) sugar
2 teaspoons ground cinnamon

Slow-Baked Spiced Quinces

SERVES 4–6

Preheat the oven to 90°C/195°F (fan-forced). Cut the lemons in half, squeeze the juice into a large bowl of water, then add the lemon halves to the bowl.

Working with one quince at a time, peel the quinces and remove the cores, reserving the peel and cores. Cut each quince into eight wedges or pieces, immediately adding them to the bowl of lemon water so they don't brown. Wrap the reserved quince scraps in a piece of muslin (cheesecloth) and secure with kitchen string.

Pour 625 ml (21 fl oz/2½ cups) water into a heavy-based saucepan. Cut the zest of the orange into wide strips, then add to the pan with the juice of the orange. Add the sugar, cinnamon sticks, vanilla seeds and pod, star anise, cloves and peppercorns.

Bring to the boil, add the muslin bag and simmer for 15 minutes, or until the liquid is syrupy. Remove the muslin bag, reserving the orange rind and spices.

Drain the quince and place in a single layer in a shallow baking dish that is just large enough to hold them. Pour the syrup over, including the reserved orange rind and spices, so the syrup comes three-quarters of the way up the side of the quince. Cut a sheet of baking paper to fit over the quince pieces, to lock in the moisture as they cook.

Transfer to the oven and bake for 8 hours, or until the quince is red and tender.

Remove the baking paper and increase the oven temperature to 120°C/250°F (fan-forced). Bake for a further 20–30 minutes, or until the syrup has reduced. Remove the spices.

Serve drizzled with the syrup, with a dollop of crème fraîche. Any leftover quince will keep in an airtight container in the fridge for several days.

3 lemons
1.5 kg (3 lb 5 oz) quinces
1 orange
440 g (1 lb/2 cups) sugar
2 cinnamon sticks
1 vanilla bean, cut in half lengthways, seeds scraped
2 star anise
4 whole cloves
6 black peppercorns
crème fraîche or thick (double/heavy) cream, to serve

Cinnamon & Orange Crème Caramels

MAKES 6

Preheat the oven to 120°C/250°F (fan-forced).

Combine the cream, milk, vanilla, cinnamon and orange peel strips in a saucepan. Bring just to the boil, then remove from the heat and allow to infuse for 10 minutes.

Place 230 g (8 oz/1 cup) of the sugar in a saucepan. Add 80 ml (2½ fl oz/⅓ cup) water and stir over medium heat until the sugar has dissolved. Increase the heat to high. Cook, without stirring, for 5–7 minutes, or until the caramel becomes dark golden, swirling the pan occasionally.

Working quickly, pour the caramel into six 185–250 ml (6½–8½ fl oz/ ¾–1 cup) ramekins or ovenproof dishes. Set aside for the caramel to set.

Place the egg yolks and eggs in a bowl and whisk in the remaining sugar. Gradually whisk in the cream mixture.

Strain the mixture into a jug, then pour the mixture into each ramekin, over the caramel. Place the ramekins in a baking dish and fill the dish with enough hot water to come halfway up the side of the ramekins.

Transfer to the oven and bake for 1 hour, or until the custards are just set. Carefully remove the ramekins from the water and allow to cool. Refrigerate for 3 hours, or until set.

To serve, run a flat-bladed knife around the inner edge of each ramekin. Place a serving plate on top of each ramekin and gently invert.

375 ml (12½ fl oz/1½ cups) thickened (whipping) cream
375 ml (12½ fl oz/1½ cups) milk
1 teaspoon vanilla extract or vanilla bean paste
1 teaspoon ground cinnamon
2 orange peel strips, about 2.5 cm (1 inch) wide, pith removed
400 g (14 oz/1¾ cups) caster (superfine) sugar
7 large free-range egg yolks
2 large free-range eggs

Dulche De Leche & Chocolate Peanut Butter Puddings

SERVES 6–8

Start by making the dulche de leche. Place the tin of condensed milk on its side in a large saucepan. Cover with water so it is submerged by at least 5 cm (2 inches). Bring to a simmer, then leave to simmer for 3 hours, topping up the water regularly so the tin remains completely submerged. Carefully remove the tin from the water. Allow to cool before opening. Spoon into a bowl and whisk until smooth. You'll only need about half the resulting dulche de leche in the pudding; the rest will keep in an airtight container for up to 5 days.

Grease a 1.5 litre (51 fl oz/6 cup) steamed pudding basin (mould) and line the base with baking paper. Beat the butter and sugar together in a bowl. Beat in the vanilla and eggs, one at a time, until fluffy and well combined. Sift the flour and cocoa powder together and mix in the chocolate melts. Fold into the egg mixture with the milk until combined. In a separate bowl, mix the dulche de leche and peanut butter together.

Spoon half the chocolate mixture into the pudding basin. Spoon in the dulche de leche mixture, then cover with the remaining chocolate mixture. Grease a sheet of baking paper and use it to cover the top of the pudding basin. Top with two layers of foil, then secure with string.

Fill a large saucepan one-third full of water and bring to the boil. Reduce the heat to a simmer. Place the pudding basing in the saucepan and cover with a lid. Gently simmer for 1 hour 20 minutes, or until a skewer inserted into the top of the pudding, through the foil, comes out almost clean, but a little fudgy.

Carefully remove the pudding from the water, then remove the string, foil and paper. Invert the pudding onto a plate. Slice into wedges and serve with thick cream.

DULCHE DE LECHE
395 g (14 oz) tin of condensed milk

PUDDING
125 g (4½ oz) butter, softened
125 g (4½ oz/⅔ cup, lightly packed) soft brown sugar
1 teaspoon vanilla extract
2 large free-range eggs
150 g (5½ oz/1 cup) self-raising flour
30 g (1 oz/¼ cup) unsweetened cocoa powder
150 g (5½ oz/1 cup) dark chocolate melts, chopped in half
125 ml (4 fl oz/½ cup) milk
180 g (6½ oz/½ cup) dulche de leche (approximately half the amount from the recipe above)
1½ tablespoons crunchy natural peanut butter (no added salt or sugar)
thick (double/heavy) cream, to serve

Index

Smith Street Books

Published in 2016 by Smith Street Books
Melbourne | Australia
smithstreetbooks.com

ISBN: 978-1-925418-09-5

CIP data is available from the National Library of Australia

Publisher: Paul McNally
Editor: Katri Hilden
Recipe development: Sue Herold, Jane O'Shannessy & Caroline Griffiths
Design concept: Kate Barraclough
Design layout: Heather Menzies, Studio31 Graphics
Photographer: Chris Middleton
Art Director & Stylist: Stephanie Stamatis
Home Economists: Sebastien Zinzan & Caroline Griffiths

Printed & bound in China by C&C Offset Printing Co., Ltd.

Book 14
10 9 8 7 6 5 4 3 2 1